D1234069

A WORKING

PEACE SYSTEM

A WORKING PEACE SYSTEM

By *DAVID MITRANY*

Introduction by *Hans J. Morgenthau*

PUBLISHED IN COOPERATION WITH
THE SOCIETY FOR
A WORLD SERVICE FEDERATION

CHICAGO 1966

QUADRANGLE BOOKS

CONTENTS

29502

INTRODUCTION

Twenty years after the end of the Second World War, the world finds itself in the grip of a gigantic paradox: we are witnessing the revival of the old, and the emergence of new forms of, nationalism in an age whose technologies of transportation, communications, and warfare have rendered nationalism in all its forms obsolete as a principle of political organization.

The revival of the traditional nationalism of the nation state, as we find it today in Europe on both sides of the Iron Curtain, is not surprising and easily understood. The old nation states of Europe barely survived the Second World War. The ravages of war and Nazism made them either dependent upon American support or exposed them to conquest by the Red Army and to Stalinist domination. If twenty years ago there had existed a supra-national framework into which they could have been fitted, the nations of Europe might well have lost their national sovereignty and be today members of a confederation or parts of an empire. Since no such framework existed or was forthcoming—the European Communities which point in that direction appeared but relatively late on the scene and have developed slowly—the nations of Europe quite naturally and perhaps inevitably used their restored strength for their traditional national purposes. The nationalism of the nations of Eastern Europe, as that of China, found an additional stimulant in the traditional fear of, and hostility to, Russia. The reassertion of nationalism became here identical with liberation from foreign domination.

A new type of nationalism, giving rise to new problems or to old ones on a greatly enlarged scale, is what Senegal's Prime Minister Mamadou Dia has called "micronationalism" creating "micronations." These are the new nations of Africa, fashioned from the fragments of the former colonial empires. Many of these new nations are lacking in one or the other or most of the attributes of nationhood. Most of them could not survive without continuous outside support. Their frontiers, being the result of the accidents of colonial policy, are frequently devoid of any kind of objective justification. Their congenital instability, as the Congo has shown, offers a standing invitation to anarchy and foreign intervention. And it is exactly this inner weakness and need for outside assistance which makes many of these new nations particularly jealous of the attributes of sovereignty and fearful of foreign intervention in the form of "neo-colonialism."

It is against the background of the revival of the old nationalism and the emergence of a new "micronationalism" that one must view the other type of nationalism, nationalistic universalism. This nationalism tries to impose a new order upon a fragmented and anarchical political world, and it does so by using its own national order as a universal model. Wilson's crusade for democracy, the "new order" of German fascism, the universal mission of Russian and Chinese Bolshevism, and the American response in the form of a commitment to protect the "free world" from it are cases in point.

The new nationalism is in truth a political religion, a nationalistic universalism which identifies the standards and goals of a particular nation with the principles that govern the universe. The few remaining nations of the first rank no longer oppose each other within a framework of shared beliefs and common values which impose effective limitations upon the means and ends of their policies. Rather they oppose each other now as the standard-bearers of moral systems, each of them of national origin and each of them claiming to provide universal moral and political standards which all the other nations ought to accept. One nation flings the challenge of its universal claim into the face of another, which reciprocates in kind.

What makes this revival, spread, and transformation of nationalism such a threat not only to the peace and order but to the very survival of the world is the fact that it is at odds with the rational requirements of the age. Modern technology has rendered the nation state obsolete as a principle of political organization; for the nation state is no longer able to perform what is the elementary function of any political organization: to protect the lives of its members and their way of life. In order to enable the state to perform that function, the feudal order, under the impact of the invention of gunpowder and of the first industrial revolution, had to yield to the dynastic and the nation state. Under the technological conditions of the pre-atomic age, the stronger nation states could, as it were, erect walls behind which their citizens could live in safety while the weaker states were protected by the operation of the balance of power, which added the resources of the strong to those of the weak.

The modern technologies of transportation, communications, and warfare, and the resultant feasibility of all-out atomic war, have completely destroyed this protective function of the nation state. No nation state is capable of protecting its citizens and their way of life against an all-out atomic attack. Its safety rests solely in preventing such an attack from taking place. While in the pre-atomic age a nation state could count upon its physical ability to defend itself, in the atomic age it must rely upon its psychological ability to deter those who are physically able to destroy it. This psychological deterrent, precarious as it is, is predicated upon the bipolarity of nuclear power; nuclear proliferation will destroy it altogether. For if more than two nations are capable of waging nuclear war, it is hazardous if not impossible to identify the aggressor for the purpose of retaliation.

It is the great paradox of our time that the age which has rendered even the great old nation states of Europe obsolete witnesses a proliferation of new nations which would not have been viable political, military, and economic entities even in the heyday of the nation state in the nineteenth century. This process of Balkanization started in the nineteenth century with the European part of the Ottoman Empire, continued with the fragmentation of the Austro-Hungarian, the western part of the Russian, and the middle-eastern part of the Turkish Empires after the First World War, and reached its climax after the Second World War with the dissolution of the colonial empires in Africa and Asia. The more enlightened statesmen of Europe and Africa are aware of the contradiction between this fragmentation and the rational requirements of the age, which call for the amalgamation of nation states into larger supra-national entities. The attempts at creating a united Europe testify to this awareness; so do many—albeit abortive—initiatives at merging a number of African states into larger units.

Similarly, the different kinds of nationalistic universalism which have sprung up since the First World War have a common purpose: to replace the present anarchy stemming from unviable fragmentation with a new world-wide system of order. What is wrong with these attempts at unifying the world is not the purpose but the method. For since at least two such political religions compete with each other, each claiming to carry the message of salvation for the world, only war could decide the issue. That is to say, the cure, being in truth an extreme manifestation of the disease of nationalism, would be worse than the disease itself.

The only rational reply to the challenge which nationalism presents to the peace and order of the world is the voluntary co-operation of a number of nations with common interests for the purpose of creating supra-national institutions after the model of the specialized agencies of the United Nations and of the European

Communities. These institutions would gradually take over the functions which the nation state has traditionally performed but is no longer able to perform today. If nation states acted in accord with the rational requirements of the age, they would strive, as it were, to make themselves superfluous. This is the "functional approach" Professor Mitrany advocates.

According to Professor Mitrany, an international community must grow from the satisfaction of common needs shared by members of different nations. International agencies, serving peoples all over the world regardless of national boundaries, could create by the very fact of their existence and performance a community of interests, valuations, and actions. Ultimately, if such international agencies were numerous enough and served the most important wants of most peoples of the earth, the loyalties to these institutions and to the international community of which they would be the agencies would supersede the loyalties to the separate national societies and their institutions.

The revival of the traditional nationalism of the nation state is in good measure a reaction to this threat to the nation state's very existence. The opposition of France to the supra-national tendencies of the European Communities is a case in point. It would be rash indeed to try to predict who will win in this contest between the old and the new, between nationalism and functionalism. But it is no exaggeration to assert that the outcome of this contest will decide the fate of the world. For nationalism as a principle of political organization is not only obsolete; but in the nuclear age it is also self-destructive. Thus the future of the civilized world is intimately tied to the future of the functional approach to international organization.

HANS J. MORGENTHAU

The University of Chicago

AUTHOR'S FOREWORD

The main essay in this collection happens to illustrate the rushing tempo, apart from the depth, of the revolutionary currents of our time. The essay was written in wartime London, when the author was working for the Foreign Office and was often at odds with his colleagues because he was apt to forecast greater political and social upheavals at the end of the war than were generally charted by official opinion. And yet, as with other papers written a little later, while it mentioned nationalist pressures in the Middle East, Southeast Asia, and elsewhere, it had no eyes for Africa. Evidently no one felt that "de-colonization" was smoldering so near below the surface, least of all in tribal Africa, the Africa which now asserts the liveliest temper and presents the most awkward problems for the international system.

Nor, more naturally, could any of us foresee in 1943 the still closer advent of the atomic bomb and nuclear guided missiles. Yet with these and satellites and space flights, and technological marvels yet to come, the whole old world of national power politics, of security through diplomatic rings and their balance of power, has been blown out of history as lightly and utterly as a cobweb in a storm. How naked in the face of all that stand the ranks of new "sovereign" states wtih their factory-fresh regalia of independence! We may go on splitting up the world into as many states as we like, but life, the inexorable product of our great scientific cunning, has by now made us all into one indivisible community, with inescapably one and the same fate—either to live or to vanish together. There is no workable dividing line between military and non-military usage of space; no means of self-protection is left, only all-round protection through some common authority.

So far, though drifting uncertainly amidst the contrary currents of social realities and sovereign assertiveness, the new nationalism has not quite denied that communality altogether. Both after 1919 and after 1945 the wartime revulsion which led to the setting up first of the League of Nations and then of the United Nations, soon eased itself back into the comforts of the years of peace; and the states drifted again into their more habitual political ways—witness the endless friction and conflict in Central and Eastern Europe after 1919, and after 1945 in the Middle East, Southeast Asia, and more lately in Africa. (A strange commentary, one might think, on the effects of radical "peacemaking.") Yet at the same time in both periods arrangements for practical international cooperation in diverse forms and directions grew in scope and range, especially since the last war. They are making a working reality of the "peaceful coexistence" which the Soviets, who had supplied the term, had meant only as a narrow police transaction.

There was a curious gloss on this at the so-called international convocation which met in New York in February 1965, to discuss the practical implications of Pope John XXIII's encyclical, *Pacem in Terris*. M. Paul-Henri Spaak, Belgian Foreign Minister, professed to see a close affinity between the call of the great Pope and Mr. Khrushchev's position. Both believed in and appealed for "peaceful coexistence," and so, according to M. Spaak, the Kremlin and the Vatican somewhat miraculously found themselves united in this humane concern. M. Spaak may have been touched by the euphoric mood of the occasion, but from someone of his standing and experience it was a strange juxtaposition, though not the less illuminating for that. Mr. Khrushchev certainly deserves credit for having faced the realities of nuclear warfare and eased Soviet policy into less dreadful channels. But he made it honestly plain—as M. Spaak himself quoted him—that for the rest East and West were to remain opposed in a "political, social, economic and cultural struggle—a struggle at every level and in every field, except that of the military."[1]

M. Spaak could not have advanced such a claim if he had heeded the oft-repeated caution of the late Justice Holmes that "one must think things, not words."[2] For while Mr. Khrushchev had in fact, if unwittingly, adopted the old view of Clausewitz that peace is only the continuation of war by other means, the Papal encyclical was expressing something fundamentally different—the sense and anxiety for a consenting world community. It was speaking for the millions within the churches and outside them who, especially since the First World War, had acknowledged the urgency of an international order cleansed of violence and arbitrary force, but who also sensed or knew that the only sure road was an international order that propagated in every possible way and direction lines of joint activity in the common service of all countries and nations. It was the point made in an essay on "The Road to Security" in 1944: that a true international society would begin to take shape when a general concern for social security would begin to loom larger than the concern for sheer military security; because "the task of statesmanship in our time is not to keep the nations peacefully apart, but to bring them actively together."[3]

[1] *On Coexistence: An Occasional Paper Resulting from an International Convocation on the Requirements of Peace,* New York, Center for the Study of Democratic Institutions of the Fund for the Republic, 1965, p. 8.

[2] No such confusion was to be found in the contribution of the Polish philosopher Adam Schaff, in spite of his Marxist persuasion (*ibid.,* p. 21). When dealing elsewhere with this very issue of abstract and particular argument, Prof. Schaff wrote "my aim was to illustrate the point that [in social matters and issues] there is no room for absolute standards, and that everything has to be assessed and broken down in relation to concrete circumstances." (*The Philosophy of Man,* New York, 1963, p. 125.)

[3] David Mitrany and others, National Peace Council, London, 1944.

That is the true, and critical, historical "confrontation" that our generation must face. As in all periods of transition both trends are at work, countering and overlapping and commanding a wavering allegiance. In spite of the protective cover of the United Nations the mass of new states, especially, has shown an uneasy sense of loneliness and has sought the shelter of fitful regional or ideological groupings. In the earlier phase the federal idea was much to the fore, and two points may be noted about that. First, with one abortive exception in East Africa and the freakish Arab schemes in the Middle East, all the schemes for federation were put forward by the old states and tried only among the new undeveloped states. Second (leaving the special case of India aside), in spite of evident common interests and the poverty of their separate resources, only one of these federal experiments survives—the uneasy union of Nigeria. We should have known from long experience with the Balkans and Latin America that local groups of unsolidified states are apt to be rent by political ambitions and jealousies which hamper even everyday cooperation among them.

The federal idea has not served any of the postwar problems and situations; nor has it suggested itself as a remedy for healing the rift between parts that had been formerly united. Some years ago the late Mr. Nehru and the Pakistani President agreed that their countries had many practical interests which could with advantage be managed in common; and now the leaders of the two parts of Ireland are working to end an old enmity by doing just that. But would either case have had a better prospect if one of the parties were to have said, "We must federate first"?[4] As for the

[4] The two leaders took the first steps almost furtively and with some fear, but both have since confessed their surprise at receiving from their peoples only proof of support and even of relief. The contrary experience has been seen in East Africa, Southeast Asia, etc., when new national governments have discarded existing common activities with neighboring states to the loss of their own peoples. Two other cases where the political has chosen to spite the social, concern the division of the waters of

grander federal designs, offering prefabricated Cities of God for the Atlantic world or even for the world at large, one can only deplore the loss they have certainly caused to constructive international action by turning popular good will, and especially student enthusiasm, in the vital postwar years into idealistic blind alleys with no effect on public action at all.

The other trend, by contrast, is earthbound, concrete, and wholly practical. In the same period non-political association and co-operation have grown quietly and undramatically, yet in ways that hold the promise of a true international community. The specialized agencies working under the United Nations have widened substantially the work started under the League of Nations; and other services and administrative links have been added to them. But the truly significant development is the vast complex of operations covered by the general term of "foreign aid" or "technical assistance" through various agencies, with the World Bank playing an outstanding part. Taken together they represent the remarkable first signs "of a sense of world community, of international responsibility for local conditions everywhere. The idea of the welfare state, new as it is even in our own countries, is already broadening out into a sentiment for a welfare world."[5] On their side the new states, politically mixed up in aggressively "uncommitted" groups

---

Kashmir between Pakistan and India, and of the waters of the Jordan among Syria, Jordan, and Israel. Fair and workable schemes had been devised by impartial agencies, and foreign aid would also have been available for carrying them out, but both have been blocked by political spite. Not only have these struggling rural populations been deprived by their own governments of the boon which nature could have given them, but instead they are suffering new burdens as in both cases the festering political antagonism is provoking military conflict. These are typical instances of how national governments deliberately prevent functional arrangements because they fear their healing effect on the outlook of their peoples.
   [5] David Mitrany, "International Co-operation in Action," *Associations* (Brussels), September 1959.

and leagues, have shown themselves eager to join the United Nations' special agencies and other such bodies "because the balance
of considerations is in favor of such participation," and they have
come to look upon it "as an international asset and a strengthening
of their position in the world." Though politically extremely sensitive, they have shown little mistrust of such bodies, "even where
the activities of the international organization within the State's
territory is concerned."[6]

Considerations such as these show why, in spite of the rash of
local political conflicts, present conditions offer both opportunity
and promise in working arrangements as a way of building a
peaceful world community. They have indeed a natural and positive basis in a new phenomenon, one neglected by students of
international affairs, in the unifying sweep of the new social philosophy. Nineteenth-century nationalism was essentially cultural,
feeding on distinctions between one people and another. The new
nationalism displays something of that but is essentially social,
with a fierce radical preoccupation with social rights. And in its
external aspect the new social philosophy has the "central characteristic that it is *universal*. I believe this to be a novel, a unique
historical situation. In the traditional categories of 'human rights'
there have always been differences from place to place in attitude,
conception, and practice. But now, whatever their constitutional
form or cultural tradition, *all* countries have adopted the philosophy and claims of social security; and hence inevitably also similar
machinery of administrative practice and controls."[7] If this reading be correct, it means that two practical elements are already at
hand, and on a world scale, to which strands of functional co-

[6] Benjamin Akzin, *New States and International Organizations*, Paris,
UNESCO, 1955, pp. 170-172.

[7] David Mitrany, Comment in the Human Rights Section, Sixth IPSA
World Conference, Geneva, September 1964.

operation could be made fast. One is the indispensable factor of a common outlook and purpose, which in this case puts into strong relief an evident identity of everyday aims and policy. The other is the useful factor of close similarity in ways and means. Administrative law is implicitly "functional" law, and so is administrative practice. It is therefore relatively simple to link them together from country to country, even if political and legal systems otherwise differ. And every functional link helps to build a common legal order—as the ILO well exemplifies—specific but also concrete and cumulative; one which does not stay aloof in the atmosphere of diplomatic pacts or juridical formulae, but which enters everywhere into the daily life of the peoples themselves.

If the ways of history at times seem as mysterious as those of the gods, it may be because its watchers have their eyes fixed on some heaven of their own imagining, rather than on the signs that mark the road below. Admittedly our time is pressed by such violent cross-currents—a political upheaval, a world-wide social revolution, and a scientific explosion which is moving beyond man's foresight and control—that its coming shape is not easy to see. We cannot know what kind of world will ultimately come out of it all. But between them the social and the scientific eruptions do seem inevitably to provide the pressures and suggest the path toward an organized world society. Only by guiding material and technical resources into joint international activities and services could we possibly hope to meet the social needs and claims of the world's surging populations, with fair provision for all. And when it comes to the new scientific inventions and discoveries, their own technicalities defy any arrangement below the global scale. Flying may still claim for awhile sovereign rights in the air above a state's territory; but with satellites and space travel we have in truth reached the "no man's land" of sovereignty. Sovereignty is nothing where it cannot be enforced.

The functional conception developed in the following pages was stated first in the William Dodge lectures given at Yale in 1932.[8] It consolidated older doubts about the fitness of traditional political constructions to safeguard the democratic content of modern society in general, much less to serve the peaceful growth of an international society in particular. That theoretical assumption was strongly confirmed by the experience of the Second World War (as indeed it had been in the great depression of the thirties). All the functional arrangements proved their worth, both in war and for reconstruction; all the federal and such political schemes proved pitifully barren. And everything that has happened since 1945 has gone the same way.

The brief speculations above suggest in a broad philosophical mood the reason why; as they suggest the extraordinary social leap which our world has made in one generation. And what for our purpose is decisive is historically also without precedent. Past seminal changes—the rise of Christianity, the industrial revolution —affected only the eastern or the western world, only a region or a continent, but now the whole of our world is enfolded in the new transformation. Is it conceivable that such a shattering and universal upheaval could be contained with the political forms and rules furnished for the parochial entity of the territorial-sovereign state— Created half to rise, and half to fall;/Great Lord of all things, yet a prey to all . . . —?

The whole critical issue was put sharply, in almost a despairing mood, in a recent article on "What Politics Is About": "At no period in history has human capacity for political creation been subjected to such continuous unremitting strain." The new inventions and discoveries "have rendered traditional ideas of 'what politics is about' almost as obsolete as astrology and alchemy. . . . In this unique historical context . . . if we are to win through, a

---

[8] *The Progress of International Government*, New Haven and London, 1933 (Chapter Three, "The Communal Organization of World Affairs").

supreme effort of political creativity is needed."[9] Even the inquiry set up by the Council of Europe itself (as mentioned below), after listening to a whole line of men in political life, could only bewail "the paucity of political inventiveness."

At least the functional ideas discussed here try to face the future; and to do so on a human practical plane, usable here and now, not having to wait on some political apocalypse.

I am grateful to the editors and publishers named in the notes to the several essays for permission to include them in this book.

[9] *The Times Literary Supplement* (London), November 18, 1965.

I
A WORKING
PEACE SYSTEM

A Working Peace System

Introduction

When this short study was first published in the summer of 1943 there was great confidence in the unity which had grown up during the war, and students of international organization were thinking mainly of how to consolidate that unity and expand it. Many of them felt that a definite constitutional framework was needed, within which the world society would grow of itself, and they naturally looked upon the ideas of this pamphlet as politically inadequate; others felt with the writer that a world society was more likely to grow through doing things together in workshop and marketplace than by signing pacts in chancelleries. Since then we have moved fast but not well. The structure of the United Nations has been erected in all its grandeur, but at the same time the practical unity of the war period threatens to fall to pieces. This uncertain situation has thrown us back again upon fundamentals. It seems best, therefore, in re-issuing this small study to leave the original argument as it stood, and in this new introduction to consider some of the ideas which have come up in the meantime.

This essay was first published by the Royal Institute of International Affairs in 1943. It was reprinted three times in England and appeared also in Italian, Norwegian, and Danish editions in 1945.

For to prefer a functional to a constitutional approach is not to be timid, much less to be haphazard. The argument has grown out of a definite view of the historical problem of our time, the chief trait of which is the baffling division between the peoples of the world. All the great religions, as well as the lay creed of humanism, have preached world unity, in the sense of a common humanity, yet after centuries of such teaching we find ourselves with little sense of such unity left in our outlook and actions. That is all the more strange since in its material life the world has moved far toward a common unity. When the sense of unity was still alive, in the Middle Ages, social life was a mosaic of small and largely self-sufficient local units; now social life has a highly integrated organic unity, but politically our outlook is bound to a mosaic of separate national units. Much depends on our understanding of this paradox now that we stand at a historical turning point. How has it come about, what does it signify in terms of world politics? Very broadly, it was bequeathed us by the dynamic nineteenth century, which internationally moved on two separate and opposite lines. Politically it saw the rise of national states, a trend which was solemnly recognized when in 1919 the Paris conference took "national self-determination" as its guiding principle and which in the Middle East, the Far East, and possibly in Africa is yet far from spent. With a new social era before us we find national states a hindrance, but historically the trend was sound in itself. It had its roots in the same currents—the Renaissance, humanism, and anti-authoritarianism—which inculcated respect for the individual personality and so, by a natural extension, also for the group or national personality. And as the first led politically to the enfranchisement of the individual, the person becoming a citizen, in the wider society the second led to the enfranchisement of national groups through states of their own. Let us call that broadly the cultural side of Western civilization. But side by side with it the same period produced a rapid and growing division of labor. The economic self-sufficiency of the individual and of the local group was broken up by the development of communications, of new sources of power, of new materials, the opening up of new lands, and the rise of mass production—and these factors have bound peoples increasingly together. That is the material side of Western civilization, and national and world trends were the same.

To reconcile these two trends is the task which history is setting us. Both are legitimate; both must be satisfied. To ignore the deep-rooted loyalties of nationality in the search for material efficiency, or to deny the swelling cry for social betterment for the sake of a fictitious independence, is to perpetuate the unrest which is the spring of perennial conflict. It is in the light of this task—of how to achieve unity in diversity (and in the domestic sphere, too, the problem is how to have planning without breaking too many individual liberties)—that we must look at the various ideas for international organization. These have followed in the main three lines of thought: (1) An association of nations, like the League, which would leave the identity and policy of states almost untouched; though comprehensive, it would be a loose association merely suggesting the need for a measure of material integration. (2) A federal system, favored because it is thought it would provide the cohesion lacking in a league; but this would be so only within the limits of some new continental or regional group and so would tend to divide the world again into a number of potentially competing units. (3) The functional approach, which seeks, by linking authority to a specific activity, to break away from the traditional link between authority and a definite territory (perpetuated by either an association or a federation of nations). This approach resolves the dilemma of creating either too loose or too narrow an international organization by building up authorities which would be comprehensive and solid, in selected fields of common life.

Practical aspects of functional organization are discussed in the body of the pamphlet. The point that matters is that whatever the form and the manner, international organization must do the same things which national governments do in modern society, only with a difference in scale. It must do those things which cannot be done well, or without friction, except on an international scale. That would mean something very different from the scope of the League of Nations. It was in keeping with our former outlook that international law in general and the Covenant in particular were concerned primarily with defining the formal relationship of states, in a negative sense, and only vaguely with initiating positive common activities. The economic, financial, and other sections of the League were mere secretariats, and so in fact is the ILO. The functional bodies contemplated here would be executive agencies with autonomous tasks and powers; they would not merely discuss but would do things for the community, and that would be in keeping with the needs of the time. The trend at present is to enlarge and co-ordinate the social scope of authority, but national planning cannot work in harness with laissez-faire in the international field. The Charter of the United Nations has at least come near to recognizing the true nature of the problem. It has entrusted to the Security Council a first definite function of common government, that of law and order; while the Economic and Social Council, though not endowed with equally definite powers, does express by its mere existence a sense that the problem of our time is not how to keep the nations peacefully apart but how to bring them actively together.

This new approach toward the goal of international collaboration is free from dogma and avoids the cramping limitations of a more nicely designed but hard-and-fast system. It is an attempt, after looking squarely at the lessons of history, to offer a practical line of action that might overcome the deep-seated division between the needs of material unity and stubborn national loyalties—a division which explains why appeals to world unity have so far remained barren and why the task is essentially one of practical statesmanship. The two obvious tests for any step toward an international order are, first, the means by which we bring about the change, and, second, the fitness of the change for the communal needs of the time. Historically two ways have been known for adapting the range of government to changing needs and aspirations—conquest and consent. The Nazi "New Order" and the Japanese "Co-Prosperity sphere" were attempts of the first kind. For us the question is how far the peoples are ripe for consent, and the answer must largely determine our line of action. If the new international experiment is to be effective it must have real tasks of government entrusted to it. But at the same time it must in its makeup accept the present reality of a world that is divided into many national states. The most one could hope for during the period of transition is that national governments should act as willing agencies of the incipient international authority; for even if it were possible to deed formal authority in full to an international body, the elements which go to the making of power—raw materials and manpower, industrial potential and strategic positions— would in the nature of things, until national boundaries and authorities are done away with altogether, still remain in the grasp of particular national groups. Nothing could be more barren and confusing, therefore, than the habit of mind which, in the words of Dr. Reinhold Niebuhr, "thinks that we lack an international government only because no one has conceived a proper blueprint of it. Therefore they produce such blueprints in great profusion. These pure constitutionalists have a touching faith in the power of a formula over the raw stuff of history."

The ultimate ideal is simple and universal. But the prospect of the first steps toward it depends not a little on whether we struggle for a formal or constitutional idea—in regard to which there are many creeds—or work for a practical achievement toward which we might strive together. Some of the issues of constitutional principle and structure which have been discussed of late show how serious can be the difference if we choose one way or the other. There is no better illustration of this than the frequent plea for a "surrender of sovereignty," and no issue has strayed farther afield from practical needs and possibilities. Sovereignty is a legal concept, a status; it cannot be surrendered unless the units which form the political community, whether individuals or groups, abdicate their political rights. Individuals have not been asked by the national state to surrender their rights as citizens, except in totalitarian dictatorships; it has never been asked of the constituent members of a federation, which would not have come into being if that had been the price. The historical process has not moved that way at all. Abrupt changes in sovereignty have occurred, but by conquest or revolution, whereas the normal way has been a gradual transfer of sovereignty according to social needs and political developments. The proof of this is that the process has moved in both directions. British colonies acquired by conquest were gradually emancipated, parts of sovereignty being *pari passu* transferred to them. Internally too, sovereignty has usually been transferred by gradual steps from autocratic kings to popular parliaments, and administrative authority from lords and estates to elected local bodies. In all this the emphasis was on political emancipation. But under the social pressures of our time the trend is now moving the opposite way, and authority is increasingly transferred from local bodies to central executives. Be that as it may, if a new world authority is to come into being by consent and not by conquest, its status will depend on how far the transfer of sovereignty from national groups is both willing and continuous.

To such willing transfers of sovereignty—or abridgment of national sovereignty—there is no limit except that set by our political maturity. But there is an effective minimum, which must include some essential functions now performed by national states. Security is first among them. There can be no real transfer of sovereignty until defense is entrusted to a common authority, because national means of defense are also means of offense and also of possible resistance to that common authority. The view that it is the function of the military arm to be the common keeper of law and order, and to that end must be under the control of a central authority, has now found a first international expression in the Security Council, and still more in the American proposals for the international control of atomic energy. Beyond this, many other tasks and activities could or should be made matters of common concern, and international society will grow precisely in the measure in which we do so join together. An editorial in *Nature* (December 1943) suggested that "functional co-operation may be a means of persuading the Powers ultimately to make the wide sacrifices in national sovereignty which the preservation of peace will demand." That is historically true and politically sound. In any normal evolution the change has been gradual—a gradual transfer of sovereignty from the ruler to the people, the people in their turn gradually entrusting its exercise to a central authority. Therefore the democratic tests have all along been expressed in a selection of policy and of ultimate control of its execution, and not in any grandiose juridical gesture. Sovereignty cannot in fact be transferred effectively through a formula, only through a function. By entrusting an authority with a certain task, carrying with it command over the requisite powers and means, a slice of sovereignty is transferred from the old authority to the new; and the accumulation of such partial transfers in time brings about a translation of the true seat of authority. If that has been the considered process in the domestic sphere, is it not still more relevant in the international sphere, where even the elements of unity have to be built up laboriously by this very process of patient change? It would indeed be sounder and wiser to speak not of the surrender but of a sharing of sovereignty. When ten or twenty national authorities, each of whom had performed a certain task for itself, can be induced to perform that task jointly, they will to that end quite naturally pool their sovereign authority insofar as the good performance of the task demands it.

This may seem a limping way toward world community. Yet eagerness for a finished constitution may actually hold up progress. It is too often overlooked that written constitutions have in the main served as a check to authority; and federal constitutions, while they serve to bind, also serve to divide. A federal system is by its nature both rigid and limiting. It arranges a few things to be done in common, but limits them strictly and also lays down the many things which must remain separate. The Indian experiment may break down on this very issue of power at the center. If that has been so in national federal states, the definition of spheres inevitably will be still more rigid at any first attempt to link up a number of states with differing political and social systems. But this is an age of potent social change. Who can foretell what the needs of social life will be a generation hence? Is it wise to open up an international era with a rigid division of tasks and authority? In the United States the effect of such constitutional division was so obstinate that in spite of a frantic crisis and the prestige of President Roosevelt the remedies of the New Deal could be set going only through political devices which bypassed the Constitution. The New Deal was a functional evolution all along the line, without any change in texts or forms, but the total effect has been to transform a loosely federal system into a highly centralized national government. The truth is that the federal idea goes in one sense too far and in another sense not far enough. Politically it is more than we can hope to obtain at present on a world scale; economically and socially it offers less than what is needed for a unified, peaceful development.

In America the functional method of change was followed not because it was easy, but because the constitutional method was well-nigh impracticable. Students of the problem realize how diffi-

cult it is to change written constitutions; they often suggest, therefore, that an international pact should provide for its periodical
revision or for its amendment by a limited vote. That was the view
which an American group circulated at the time of the United
Nations Assembly in the spring of 1946. It proposed that the
Assembly should be able to pass amendments by a two-thirds
majority, the vote being weighted, and that these amendments
should take effect when ratified by a majority of members of the
United Nations. It is strange that such neat schemes should be put
forward by American students who must know what a hard and
ungrateful task it is to try to amend the Constitution in their own
united country. It rarely succeeds, but it often brings up again
issues and feelings which had lain dormant and so, if anything,
hardens the existing political division. Clearly it would be much
more difficult in the case of an international constitution. The
experience of the League and of the ILO has been that even when
amendments are accepted by the international bodies they are
rarely ratified by the governments concerned, not merely because
they are sovereign states but because the very purpose of a formal
constitution is as much to prevent change as it was to bring it
about originally. Too many changes would alter the balance of
power in a federal system, as all new functions allotted to the
central authority would have a cumulative effect on its power;
under a functional system that power would be distributed and
dispersed. But this apart, most of the tasks before us are not
formal issues, such as the rights of man, but practical tasks in the
nature of social services. They need practical co-operation rather
than formal submission to the will of a majority. When it is a
matter of willing and active participation, formal amendment of
established compacts is not the best way to make progress.

The same uneasiness as to how a formal compact is to be made
to work crops up in another demand—that we should have a
league not of governments but of peoples. In a debate in the House

of Commons[1] it was urged, for instance, that any international assembly should be composed of representatives popularly elected, preferably by the national parliaments. These ideas may be pleasing to the democratic eye, but can they be made into a working instrument of world government? Whom would such an assembly represent, and who would carry out the measures passed by it? If it has any sense at all the idea must intend that assembly to develop an outlook of its own, but if on any important issue it should come to differ from the view of national parliaments, which is to prevail? Either the world assembly must have authority to impose its will, or its decisions would remain perhaps admirable but nonetheless pious opinions. Sovereignty in any comprehensive sense cannot lie at the same time with a world assembly and with national parliaments. Indeed, the more popular the basis of representation of a world assembly the less real power is likely to be granted it at the first. A report of the ILO Committee on constitutional questions said that "the preponderant view of the Committee was that a weakening of the Government vote (by changing the balance of the tri-partite delegations) would lessen the regard given to decisions of the Conference, and might seriously impair its authority as a quasi-legislative or pre-legislative body." Obviously there is here a confusion of two aims, both of them legitimate but neither helped by being mixed with the other. One aim is to create a forum for the expression of progressive world opinion; the other aim is to build up an effective instrument of common policy. The two functions are not identical, and an assembly which was over-zealous in the first would become ineffective in the second. And in general, if to the inevitable differences between states are to be added differences between governments and their own national representatives, the prospect of any tangible work coming out of a world assembly would be very dim indeed.

The two main objects of government are the organization of stability and the organization of change. As regards the first, it

[1] Hansard, House of Commons, January 28, 1946.

would not be difficult constitutionally, if the political will were there, to translate the instruments and experience of national life into the needs of an international order; but with regard to peaceful change the problem in the two spheres is utterly different. All the efforts to devise an international system, all the demands for restraining national sovereignty, center upon this issue of how to bring about the voluntary and progressive evolution of world society. The weakness of the League of Nations lay in the fact that it was limited to the task of organizing stability. In this respect the United Nations Charter shows a great advance, and it is significant that the changes which at San Francisco were made in the original draft all tended to add weight to the economic and social functions of the new international organization. But in a field which is so vast and complex and in which the participants are so different in outlook and levels of organization, common ways of thinking and of doing things will not be easy to achieve. Here again the demand for equity tribunals and such devices has only served to confuse the problem; even the legislative process to which we are accustomed in the West may prove at first an uncertain instrument. The choice we shall have to make at every point will be between a gratifying form and the effective working of the international experiment. If, for instance, the immediate problem is how to bring power under some common control, it is as well to admit that it cannot be done without the willing partnership of the Great Powers themselves. Their preponderance is inevitable; the only choice is between power exercised within a common organization—for defined common ends and under a measure of common control—or independently and arbitrarily from without. The smaller and weaker states would be well rewarded if in return for some limitation on the formal principle of equality—which at best has never been more than a political fiction—they could get an assurance of peace and a growing measure of social equality through the working of international services.

Certain it is that power cannot be restrained except within an effective world system; and to be effective, indeed to come about at all, such a system will have to be built up not on tenets of formal equality but on such as would satisfy the one crucial question: How can we make this organization work and last? The transition from national to international control of power is bound to be stubborn. It is not an unprincipled or an unwise compromise to err, if need be, on the side of working democracy rather than of voting democracy.

The General Problem

The need for some new kind of international system was being widely canvassed before the Second World War, in the measure in which the League of Nations found itself frustrated in its attempts to prevent aggression and to organize peace. Some blamed this failure on the irresponsibility of small states; others rather the egoism of the Great Powers. Still others imputed the League's failure more directly to weaknesses in its own constitution and machinery: the proper ingredients were there, but the political dosage was inadequate. It was especially among those who held this view that the idea of a wide international federation began to be embraced as a new hope.

Federation seemed indeed the only alternative to a League tried so far for linking together a number of political units by democratic methods. It would mean an association much closer than was the League, and its advocacy therefore takes it for granted that the League failed because it did not go far enough. In what way would federation go further? Federation would be a more intensive union of a less extensive group; the constitutional ties would be closer. Second, certain activities would be more definitely and actively tied together. More definite common action is clearly the end; the formal arrangements which the federalists put in the forefront would be merely a necessary adjunct, to ensure the reliable working of the federal undertakings. And that is as it should be for, leaving formal arguments aside, it is plain that the League failed not from overstrain but from inanition. It might have done more about sanctions, but that would not have been enough. Even if the League's action for "security" had been more fearless that would not by itself have sufficed to give vitality to an international system that was to last and grow. To achieve that end, such a system must in some important respects take over and co-ordinate activities hitherto controlled by the national state, just as the state increasingly has to take over activities which until now have been carried on by local bodies; and like the state, any new international authority could under present conditions not be merely a police authority.

We realize now that the League failed because, whatever the reasons, it could not further that process of continuous adjustment and settlement which students of international affairs call "peaceful change." But they themselves, taking the form for the substance, all too often thought of it mainly as a matter of changing frontiers. We shall have to speak of this again, but what peaceful change should mean, what the modern world, so closely interrelated, must have for its peaceful development, is some system that would make possible automatic and continuous social action, continually adapted to changing needs and conditions, in the same sense and of the same general nature as any other system of government. Its character would be the same for certain purposes; only the range would be new. It is in that sense that the League's work has in truth been inadequate and ineffective, as one may readily see if one reflects whether a change of frontiers now and then would really have led to a peaceful and co-operative international society.

A close federation is supposed to do just what the League proved unable to do, and in a set and solid way. But to begin with, can we take a system which has worked well in one field and simply transplant it to another, so much wider and more complex? Federations have still been national federations; the jump from national states to international organization is infinitely more hazardous than was the jump from provincial units to national federations. None of the elements of neighborhood, of kinship, of history are there to serve as steps. The British Empire is bound closely by old ties of kinship and history, but no one would suggest that there is among its parts much will for federation. Yet apart from this matter of whether the federal idea has any great prospects, there is the more important question whether it would have any great virtues in the international sphere. If the evil of conflict and war springs from the division of the world into detached and competing political units, will it be exorcised simply by changing or reducing the lines of division? Any political reorganization into separate units must sooner or later produce the same effects; any international system that is to usher in a new world must produce the opposite effect of subduing political division. As far as one can see, there are only two ways of achieving that end. One would be through a world state which would wipe out political divisions forcibly; the other is the way discussed in these pages, which would rather overlay political divisions with a spreading web of international activities and agencies, in which and through which the interests and life of all the nations would be gradually integrated. That is the fundamental change to which any effective international system must aspire and contribute: to make international government co-extensive with international activities. A League would be too loose to be able to do it; a number of sectional federations would, on the contrary, be too tight to be welded into something like it. Therefore when the need is so great and pressing, we must have the vision to break away from traditional political ideas, which in modern times have always linked authority to a given territory, and try some new way that might take us without violence toward that goal. The beginnings cannot be anything but experimental; a new international system will need, even more than national systems, a wide freedom of continuous adaptation in the light of experience. It must care as much as possible for common needs that are evident, while presuming as little as possible upon a global unity which is still only latent and unrecognized. As the late John Winant well said in a lecture at Leeds in October 1942: "We must be absolute about our principal ends (justice and equality of opportunity and freedom), relative and pragmatic about the mechanical means used to serve those ends."

The need for a pragmatic approach is all the greater because we are so clearly in a period of historical transition. When the state itself, whatever its form and constitution, is everywhere undergoing a deep social and political sea-change, it is good statesmanship not to force the new international experiments into some set familiar form, which may be the less relevant the more respectable it seems, but to see above all that these experiments go with and fit into the general trend of the time.

When one examines the general shape of the tasks that are facing us one is, to begin with, led to question whether order could be brought into them by the device of formal written pacts. Why did written constitutions, declarations of rights, and other basic charters play such a great role during the nineteenth century? The task of that time, following the autocratic period, was to work out a new division of the sphere of authority, to determine new relationships between the individual and the state, to protect the new democracy. These relationships were meant to be fixed and final, and they had to rest on general principles, largely of a negative character. It was natural and proper that all that should be laid down in formal rules, meant to remain untouched and permanent. In much the same way the new nation-state was in world society what the new citizen was in municipal society; and with the increase in their number, the liberal growth in international trade and cultural and social intercourse, the resulting international rules and a host of written treaties and pacts sought, like the national constitutions, to fix the formal relationship between the sovereign individual states and their collectivity; which in this case also was expected to be fixed and final, with international law as a gradually emerging constitution for that political cosmos.

Viewed in this light, the Covenant of the League is seen to have continued that nineteenth-century tradition. It was concerned above all with fixing in a definite way the formal relationship of the member states and in a measure also of non-members, and only in a very secondary way with initiating positive common activities and action. The great exception, security, was a vital action, but a negative one; its end was not to promote the active regular life of the peoples but only to protect it against being disturbed. Broadly one might say that the Covenant was an attempt to universalize and codify the rules of international conduct, gradually evolved through political treaties and pacts, and to give them general and permanent validity. It was neither unnatural nor unreasonable to follow up that nineteenth-century trend and try to steady international relations by bringing them within the framework of a written pact, one provided with set rules for its working. But when it came to going beyond that, the League could not be more or do more than what its leading members were ready to be and do, and they were ready to do but little in a positive way. It was indeed characteristic of the post-Armistice period 1918-19 that even the victors hastened to undo their common economic and other machinery, such as the Allied Shipping Control, which had grown and served them well during the war. And that was at a time when within each country government action and control were spreading fast, causing many a private international activity also to be cut down or cut off. In other words, the incipient common functions, as well as many old connections, were disbanded in the international sphere at the very time when a common constitution was being laid down for it. It was that divorce between life and form that doomed the League from the outset, and not any inadequacy in its written rules.

Hence it is pertinent to ask: Would another written pact, if only more elaborate and stringent, come to grips more closely with the problems of our time? Let us by way of a preliminary answer note two things: First, the lusty disregard for constitutions and pacts, for settled rules and traditional rights, is a striking mark of the times. In the pressure for social change no such formal ties are allowed to stand in the way, either within the several countries or between them. It is a typical revolutionary mood and practice. If it does not always take the outward form of revolution that is because the governments themselves act as spearheads of the trend, and not only in countries ruled by dictatorships. Those who lead in this rush for social change pride themselves indeed on their disregard for forms and formalities. The appeal which communism, fascism, and nazism had for youth in particular and for the masses in general lies in no small degree in that political iconoclasm. At the turn of the nineteenth century the radical masses were demanding settled rules and rights, and Napoleon could play the trump card of constitutional nationalism against the autocratic rulers. Now the masses demand social action without regard to established "rights," and the totalitarian leaders have been playing the strong card of pragmatic socialism against constitutional democracy.

That universal pressure for social reform, in the second place, has utterly changed the relation of nationalism to internationalism, in a way that could be promising if rightly used. In constitution-making there was a parallel between the two spheres, but nothing more, for they belonged politically to different categories. The nineteenth-century nationalism rested mainly on cultural and other differentiating factors, and the creation of the nation state meant inevitably a breaking up of world unity. A cosmopolitan outlook

spread rapidly, but the nations at the same time balked at international political organization and control, and they could justify
that refusal by seemingly good principle. At present the new nationalism rests essentially on social factors; these are not only alike
in the various countries, thus paradoxically creating a bond even
between totalitarian groups, but often cannot make progress in
isolation. At many points the life of the nation state is overflowing
back into that common world which existed before the rise of
modern nationalism. At present the lines of national and international evolution are not parallel but converging, and the two
spheres now belong to the same category and differ only in dimensions.

In brief, the function of the nineteenth century was to restrain
the powers of authority; that led to the creation of the "political
man" and likewise of the "political nation," and to the definition
through constitutional pacts of their relation to the wider political
group. The Covenant (and the Locarno and Kellogg pacts) was
still of that species essentially, with the characteristic predominance of rules of the "thou shalt not" kind. The function of our
time is rather to develop and co-ordinate the social scope of authority, and that cannot be so defined or divided. Internationally it
is no longer a question of defining relations between states but of
merging them—the workaday sense of the vague talk about the
need to surrender some part of sovereignty. A constitutional pact
could do little more than lay down certain elementary rights and
duties for the members of the new community. The community
itself will acquire a living body not through a written act of faith
but through active organic development. Yet there is in this no
fundamental dispute as to general principles and ultimate aims.
The only question is, which is the more immediately practicable
and promising way: whether a general political framework should
be provided formally in advance, on some theoretical pattern, or
left to grow branch by branch from action and experience and so
find its natural bent.

The Perplexities of Federation

Perhaps as good a way as any to seek an answer to that question, essential as a starting point, is to examine some of the main aspects and implications of the schemes proposed. During the war it had been widely suggested that a federal scheme alone can meet our need, and a number of actual schemes have been put on paper. How effective would these federal schemes be, and where would they lead us politically? Before examining more definite aspects, however, it would be well to look in passing at one or two of the general propositions in which those schemes are often wrapped. As is the way of wrappings, they only obscure the substance of the contents, but these general propositions help to reveal the conception which lies behind the schemes and so its fitness for our needs.

One of the most persistent of these propositions is the attempt to distinguish between a union of peoples as against a union of states. Federation, it is insisted, must be a union of peoples, to escape the "fundamental flaw in the League in its being made of States as members." We must refrain from indulging in the nice speculation as to what, under this conception, is the state; and of how the state would be separated from the people and the people detached from their state. We must take the federalists on their own ground, which claims that to create something good and lasting we must unite not the chief political units but the several political societies—the peoples—themselves. What peoples, one is led to ask, and how? Clearly, they must be united as whole communities. We cannot pick and choose parts of them; we must take the whole of each nation as now organized, with its groups and sections, without discriminating between classes and parties and so on. That means that we include not only those who believe in the union but also those—who assuredly must exist, if only as a minority—who do not; and given the democratic process, that minority may at any time become a majority. What will happen to the union of peoples if some of the new majorities begin to tug at the common bonds? A union of peoples means, in effect, the union of political groups, and these and their attitudes are bound to alter, or could be made to alter easily with the powerful means for stirring up mass sentiments which are now available. Here again there is the same harking back to the outlook and conditions of the nineteenth century, when "popular" was supposed to be all that was fair and reliable. Now that we have had some experience of what totalitarian dictators can do with popular opinion, either by usurping it or by corrupting it, we must look for some foundation that is not so easily changed by propaganda or shattered if abused by some particular group or unit.

That concern with dogmatic forms and appearances comes out still more strongly in the basis suggested for selecting the federal members. There are only two criteria of selection: one essentially geographical, the other essentially ideological, in the broader sense of that term. A Pan-American or European federation would be of the first type and would cut across ideological divisions; an Anglo-Saxon or a "democratic" federation would be of the second type and would cut across natural geographical divisions. What would be the effects and implications of these alternatives?

Continental Unions. There was much talk in the late 1930's of the need for "continental" unions. The Germans argued for a Monroe Doctrine for Europe and the Japanese for one for Asia, while in the home of that doctrine Pan-Americanism has grown some fresh roots. Americans naturally denounced the distortion of their doctrine by Nazi and Japanese. The Monroe Doctrine was meant to protect the states of the Americas, not to subject them to the strongest among them; the factor which has been and remains the chief obstacle to Pan-Americanism, fear of domination by the major partner, Germany and Japan regarded as the proper condition for a continental union. Such a demand is itself almost proof that there was no real unity in Europe or Asia, as there was little in the Western Hemisphere. Yet it is a realistic anticipation of a relationship that would be well-nigh inevitable in existing circumstances, until the factor of power shall have been tamed; and the closer the union the more inevitably would it be dominated by the more powerful member. That is a first objection to schemes for continental union.

In the second place, the "Roman" peace within such unions, even if tolerable to those subject to it, in no way promises to be also a contribution to world peace. One of the most constant lessons of political experience suggests that such aggregations would be flushed with a new sense of power, as they would be provided with a greater ability to use it. A few years ago, when the Pan-European idea was more in fashion, its chief exponent had a fleeting moment of intuitive sincerity. The Pan-European movement, wrote Count Coudenhove-Kalergi, "is not a movement for world peace but for union, similar to the movements for German and Italian union in the nineteenth century. The movements for union were inwardly also movements for peace." But outwardly? The German Empire was not satiated when it had united the congeries of small Germanic states. A full-fledged Pan-American union would at best be strongly isolationist. There is little promise of peace in the mere change from the rivalry of Powers and alliances to the rivalry of whole continents, tightly organized and capable of achieving a high degree of, if not actual, self-sufficiency. Continental unions would have a more real chance than individual states to practice the autarky that makes for division.

Yet without that promise of peace such unions could not bring with them a promise of continued social well-being. But there is in any case no assurance—and that is the third objection—that a European federation especially would bring its peoples prosperity. Schemes of this kind have been mooted more than once in earlier years, but then Europe was in effect the political stage of the world. Economic relations with the rest of the world were yet modest, and so was general intercourse; communications were clumsy, the exchange of goods and ideas was limited, and Europe was, and felt, much of a unit *vis-à-vis* a vast, exotic outer world. Since then powerful centers of social life have developed also in the other continents, and that has led not to segregation but to an ever greater and varied economic and social interdependence of all peoples and lands. What therefore might have amounted to a fairly self-contained international, if European, society if those earlier plans had been adopted, in our time would mean rather the cutting up of a somewhat loose but living world system. The advocates of continental unions have often argued that a universal system would skip a stage in the political evolution of the world. "Just as the idea of national unity was a postulate of the nineteenth century," wrote Kalergi, "so is the idea of continental unity a postulate of the twentieth century." The analogy is more revealing than valid. There is a fictitious naturalness about these continental units. None of them has in fact that unity of type and purpose which drew men of one nation together, and if such unions would tie up certain strands they would tear up many more, and more promising ones. The problems which now divide the national states would almost all crop up again in any territorial realignment; their dimensions would be different, but not their evil nature. Yet if the analogy is fallacious, its use is significant. It shows that those who use it cannot break away from the conception which can see political society only as territorially closed units, aiming at being politically and economically self-contained. Insofar as they have to admit that existing limits are holding up social progress—though their concern is admittedly more with military security—they can think merely of stretching that conception but not of going beyond it or outside it.

Ideological Unions. Since the battle of the ideologies, which has played havoc with the League, a different type of federation has been urged upon us—not a geographical but what one might call a sympathetic federation, with as a conspicuous example Mr. Streit's first proposal for the federation of fifteen democracies. This criterion of selection would obviate the evident lack of unity of outlook of continental unions, but it assumes in the countries concerned a democratic unity which is seldom there. It would abandon to their fate democratic sections in the states excluded, while taking in, in the states included, non-democratic sections which would be a weakness in, and a latent threat to, the new body politic. The French Canadians are one example of such discordant groups, and such dissident minorities, as we have said, may at times become majorities. France, which was to be one of the pillars of Mr. Streit's scheme, is a somewhat different case in point. What would happen if one or more members were to go fascist and so lose their qualification for membership? And what if, at the same time, countries formerly fascist were to go democratic? Would the first be turned out and the second taken in? Federation under present conditions means a fairly close organization, political and economic; to revise the membership perhaps every few years would mean to disrupt periodically those very factors which are the life-blood of any union. Or if that is to be avoided and the original union kept together, either its ideological basis would have to be jettisoned or it would have to be maintained by force. That would almost turn the union into a Holy Alliance which would be led to stifle the democratic process in the house of its members in order to keep up the democratic dogma in its own constitution.

Like the idea of continental unions, such ideological exclusivism is not a new thing. The great radicals who during the revolutionary period of the nineteenth century pleaded for the federation of Europe had one trait in common: they were all republicans, and the one point on which they insisted was that only "free" peoples should be admitted into the federation. The congress over which Victor Hugo presided laid down the conditions of freedom as consisting of freedom of the press and association, universal suffrage, and control over taxation—all of them matters of internal organization. The advocates of federation were really concerned with the state, not with the world, being convinced that rivalries and conflicts between nations were all the work of princes. Their ideological successors now hold the national state to be the culprit, but they still expect salvation from the mere existence of parliament and parties, and peace to flow from the scroll of free constitutions. Which is the truth—that we cannot have an international society until the peoples are free, or that the peoples cannot be free until we have an international society? It is at least arguable that national society might not have come into being if the component parts had been expected to become democratic first. In any case we can hardly take that stand now, even if in the middle of the nineteenth century it was not unreasonable. The reformers of the time were concerned with the organization of the state, in its constitutional basis; we are concerned with the organization of the world, in its active working relations. The purpose of any new international system would be to regulate the politics of its common life, not the parochial politics of its members. To try to do this would be to inject ideological issues with a vengeance into the whole system, whereas the evident need is precisely to neutralize them. It is a task of practical government, not of political baptism.

Moreover, while we must refrain from speculating on the nice question of definition, revealing though that might be, we cannot avoid it altogether, as it must form the basis for selecting the members. In pre-war Europe and the Americas there was many a country whose written constitution was all that a democrat could wish. Would that political facade qualify for a place in a democratic union? In the second place, the reference here is generally to political democracy. What of the claim of the Left that capitalism is the mischief-maker and that only social democracy could bring peace? If political democracies should hold that peace demands the exclusion of fascist states, the socialists within them might claim that peace demands the social transformation of the democracies first. Both the political democrats and the social democrats would take their stand on what would be really issues of national organization, either equally valid or equally invalid for our purpose, and on that ground there is no reconciling them. Clearly, there is here a gross but fundamental confusion as to the real issue involved. The criterion of selection is made to rest on existing or professed democratic form, whereas the only test that could satisfy is that of democratic performance. And the performance that matters, in this as in the life of any other group, is that related to the purpose of the grouping and covering the extent of its mutal relationships. It does not matter to a football team that one of its slackers is otherwise a good engineer, efficient and reliable in his engineering relations; and it does not matter to a group of engineers that one of its failures is a good and efficient member of his local friendly society. The performance which matters in international affairs is that which concerns and affects the sphere of international relations. A democratic federation would not lead to peace if some of its members, while democratically governed, were in the wider sphere to break the rules of democratic conduct. Abyssinia was assailed by fascist Italy, but it was democratic Italy that laid hands on Tripoli and the Dodecanese; and a presumably democratic Poland it was that seized Vilna. Some other countries, though not democratically governed according to current definition, like Portugal, or Turkey under Kemal, may behave democratically in their international relations. Which of the two would make the better constituent of a democratic international union?

In the years immediately before the war the U.S.S.R. was more ready to uphold the League's system of security than many a democratic member, while she had no part in the work of the ILO. Japan, on the other hand, remained a member of the ILO even after she had resigned from the League. Should they have been excluded from what they were willing to do because they were not doing everything else? This is another aspect of the same question, cases of a partial sharing in international action, which shows how difficult it must be, and even damaging, to insist on orthodoxy. In every case what matters is a readiness to co-operate for avoiding conflict and for advancing the task of common well-being. That is all one can ask and all one need ask. The very end of political organization is to make it possible that people with differing views and divergent sentiments should yet work together peacefully for common ends. Law and order have never meant a mere declaration of faith, but a line of conduct. In national society life is divided into public and private spheres; even in the public sphere the citizen may hold and speak any views as long as he does not willfully obstruct its course, i.e., as long as he behaves democratically. That dichotomy is a fundamental trait of liberal democracy; it is totalitarian doctrine that denies the right to a difference of outlook, even in matters not of common concern. Nor is it otherwise in existing federations. There is much variation in the several parts of the United States in regard to press and censorship, the right of meeting and association, franchise qualifications, etc. More recently the intent and spirit of the federal labor laws have been greatly cramped by restrictive legislation in a score of states, nor would anyone claim that the states of the cotton belt are governed democratically. Farther north, Quebec shows many a democratic flaw, while Alberta has in a different direction tried to go a way of her own. Yet in both countries federal activities are developing fast and progressively; it would indeed be true to say that it is in the widening of that common field that the democratic process is best satisfied and expressed. What justification is there for expecting more and asking more in international society? If anything, our initial demands must be more modest there, both because international bonds are more tenuous and because innate differences between the parts are more marked and more sensitive.

Clearly, the ideological criterion of selection, in any case difficult to define, would be as invidious in operation as it is irrelevant in principle.

Common Defects of Sectional Unions. While territorial or continental groupings, therefore, would lean upon an unreal unity of outlook and interest, ideological groupings would cut across certain real and natural interests. In Europe, and still more in the Western Hemisphere, they would break up, for instance, what are in effect natural units for security, and so would tend to grow the habits of a grand alliance rather than of a collective system of law and order.

Apart from such particular defects all sectional schemes have certain defects in common. What, above all, would be their relations with outside groups and their effect upon them? Pan-Europa, as we know, was in practice to be a separate organization, with a point directed against Russia and one against the United States. A "democratic" federation would of set purpose have a point against non-democratic Powers, just as the Nazi-Fascist Axis, in spite of the Anti-Comintern Pact, was led by its ideology to turn rather against the liberal democratic states. The first effect of any such sectional grouping, therefore, must be to force those left outside to join together in some counter-group. "Such seems the disposition of man," said Dr. Johnson, "that whatever makes a distinction produces rivalry." Continental unions would almost have to invent extraneous danger or antagonism so as to stimulate internal unity; ideological unions would, of course, have such bogies ready-made. We should be thrown back upon a balance of power between groups that would be much more formidable than those which broke the back of the European Concert in 1914, or than the Axis and counter-Axis groups of the 1930's.

To obviate that danger, those who realize it propose that sectional unions should be linked up into a wider association, probably a universal League. But the mere fact of association will not lay the danger; it will all depend on the nature of the sectional units and on their relation to the wider body. Now, federal schemes imply a fairly close organization of joint activities and interests of member states. Security, economic and social development, all require under present conditions, whatever the unit of organization, centralized planning and control. The closer the organization of the sectional unions, the sharper will be their division from other similar unions and the more tenuous their links with any universal body. It is useless to hope and to prescribe that relations with other groups should be liberal and co-operative. Finance, production, defense, etc., cannot be organized tightly in a sectional unit and at the same time be open on equal terms to other units. Even so relatively mild a step as the Ottawa preferential arrangement helped to divide the British Empire from the rest of the world; while in the opposite sense the close economic ties which are growing up now between Canada and America, should they persist after the war in their present limited character, would loosen in a corresponding degree Canada's ties with the Empire. The organization of a federal group would have to be rigid, and therefore so will be its relations with other similar units. It is not possible to change the structure of such planned economy, or system of defense, continuously; therefore the closer federal unit would in fact be the active dominant unit in political and social life, inevitably with privileges for its members and restrictions against non-members. Insofar as successful it would engender a group patriotism, thus in the end reproducing in all political essentials the relationship which has existed between states and the League rather than that between a state and its local bodies, or that of a federation to its members. The center of gravity of the new international life, that is, would again be misplaced unless the scope and authority of the smaller units were to be correspondingly lesser than those of the wider grouping—and in that case they could not be close federations.

Between the conception of a universal league or association and that of sectional unions there is, therefore, a difference not merely of degree but of essence. The sectional units would proceed in the old way through a definition of a limited territory, the other through the organization of certain common interests; and while the first would organize within their limits with the inevitable tendency to differentiate between members and outsiders, the second would select and organize certain activities for the opposite purpose of integrating with regard to them the interests and actions of all.[2] That is precisely the urgent task which is facing us and which will test the effectiveness of any new international system: to make international government co-extensive with international activities. That, as we shall see, happens to be also the only way for developing among nations an order of genuine equality, based upon a sharing of positive rights and duties, in lieu of the present legal fiction which has hampered co-operation without providing security. When the League considered the idea of regional groups, as in the Geneva Protocol, it was clearly laid down that regional pacts must be open to all who might wish to join them. Pan-Americanism has not been a barrier to a wider international system, much less a substitute for it, as was shown by the participation of many Latin-American states in the League; indeed, unless a wider system were to come into being the reluctance of some Latin-American states to being tied to a Pan-American system might increase. The apparent affinity between such regional bodies and federal unions only serves to bring into relief the real disparity

[2] The idea is perfectly described in the definition of a "region" proposed by the U.S. National Resources Planning Board—roughly, that a region is the *locus* of a problem, its limits the limit of that problem, with a focal center for its administration. On that definition America has some 112 different regional systems—one for the Federal Reserve Bank, one for the Agricultural Adjustment Administration, and so on—for different federal purposes. Some coincide with state boundaries, others do not, and their administrative centers are in different parts and cities.

between the two conceptions. In the League the regional groups were meant to be a means for administrative devolution; in the other they would be a means for political exclusion. A state could fit naturally into the several parts of a system of international devolution, but it could not be on equal terms both a member of a sectional union and of a universal association. Close sectional unions would in effect represent merely a rationalized nationalism, with wider limits for the individual units but otherwise reproducing the working characteristics of the system of national states.

The Functional Alternative

Can these vital objections be met, and the needs of peace and social advance be satisfied, through some other way of associating the nations for common action? The whole trend of modern government indicates such a way. That trend is to organize government along the lines of specific ends and needs, and according to the conditions of their time and place, in lieu of the traditional organization on the basis of a set constitutional division of jurisdiction and of rights and powers. In national government the definition of authority and the scope of public action are now in a continuous flux, and are determined less by constitutional norms than by practical requirements. The instances are too many and well known to need mentioning; one might note only that while generally the trend has been toward greater centralization of services, and therefore of authority, under certain conditions the reverse has also occurred, powers and duties being handed over to regional and other authorities for the better performance of certain communal needs. The same trend is powerfully at work in the several federations, in Canada and Australia, and especially in the United States, and in these cases it is all the more striking because the division of authority rests on written constitutions which are still in being and nominally valid in full. Internationally, too, while a body of law had grown slowly and insecurely through rules and conventions, some common activities were organized through *ad hoc* functional arrangements and have worked well. The rise of such specific administrative agencies and laws is the peculiar trait, and indeed the foundation, of modern government.

A question which might properly be asked at the outset in considering the fitness of that method for international purposes is this: Could such functions be organized internationally without a comprehensive political framework? Let it be said, first, that the functional method as such is neither incompatible with a general constitutional framework nor precludes its coming into being. It only follows Burke's warning to the sheriffs of Bristol that "government is a practical thing" and that one should beware of elaborating constitutional forms "for the gratification of visionaries." In national states and federations the functional development is going ahead without much regard to, and sometimes in spite of, the old constitutional divisions. If in these cases the constitution is most conveniently left aside, may not the method prove workable internationally without any immediate and comprehensive constitutional framework? If, to cite Burke again, it is "always dangerous to meddle with foundations," it is doubly dangerous now. Our political problems are obscure, while the political passions of the time are blinding. One of the misfortunes of the League experiment was that a new institution was devised on what have proved to be outworn premises. We might also recollect that of the constitutional changes introduced in Europe after the First World War, fine and wise though they may have been, none has survived even a generation. How much greater will that risk of futility be in Europe after the Second World War, when the split within and between nations will be much worse than in 1919? We know now even less about the dark historical forces which have been stirred up by the war, while in the meantime the problems of our common society have been distorted by fierce ideologies which we could not try to bring to an issue without provoking an irreconcilable dogmatic conflict. Even if action were to be to some extent handicapped without a formal political framework, the fact is that no obvious sentiment exists, and none is likely to crystallize for some years, for a common constitutional bond.

In such conditions any pre-arranged constitutional framework would be taken wholly out of the air. We do not know what, if anything, will be in common—except a desperate craving for peace and for the conditions of a tolerable normal life. The peoples may applaud declarations of rights, but they will call for the satisfaction of needs. That demand for action could be turned into a historic opportunity. Again we might take to heart what happened in the U.S. in 1932–33 and think of what chances the Roosevelt administration would have had to achieve unity, or indeed to survive, if instead of taking immediate remedial action it had begun by offering constitutional reforms—though a common system was already in being. A timid statesman might still have tried to walk in the old constitutional grooves; Mr. Roosevelt simply stepped over them. He grasped both the need and the opportunity for centralized practical action. Unemployment, the banking collapse, flood control, and a hundred other problems had to be dealt with by national means if they were to be dealt with effectively and with lasting results.

The significant point in that emergency action was that each and every problem was tackled as a practical issue in itself. No attempt was made to relate it to a general theory or system of government. Every function was left to generate others gradually, like the functional subdivision of organic cells; and in every case the appropriate authority was left to grow and develop out of actual performance. Yet the new functions and the new organs, taken together, have revolutionized the American political system. The federal government has become a national government, and Washington for the first time is really the capital of America. In the process many improvements in the personnel and machinery of government have come about, and many restrictive state regulations have melted away. More recently there has been heard the significant complaint that the ties between cities and their states are becoming looser, while those with the national government become ever stronger. No one has worked to bring this about, and no written act has either prescribed it or confirmed it. It has been a purely functional development at every point. A great constitutional transformation has thus taken place without any changes in the Constitution. There have been complaints, but the matter-of-course acceptance has been overwhelming. People have gladly accepted the service when they might have questioned the theory. The one attempt at direct constitutional revision, to increase and liberalize the membership of the Supreme Court, was bitterly disputed and defeated. Yet that proposal involved in effect much less of a constitutional revolution than has the experiment of the Tennessee Valley Authority. The first would not have ensured any lasting change in the working of American government, whereas the second has really introduced into the political structure of the United States a new regional dimension unknown to the Constitution.

In many of its essential aspects—the urgency of the material needs, the inadequacy of the old arrangements, the bewilderment in outlook—the situation at the end of the Second World War will resemble that in America in 1933, though on a wider and deeper scale. And for the same reasons the path pursued by Mr. Roosevelt in 1933 offers the best, perhaps the only, chance for getting a new international life going. It will be said inevitably that in the United States it was relatively easy to follow that line of action because it was in fact one country, with an established Constitution. Functional arrangements could be accepted, that is, because in many fields the federal states had grown in the habit of working together. That is no doubt true, but not the most significant point

of the American experiment; for that line was followed not
because the functional way was so easy but because the constitutional way would have been so difficult. Hence the lesson for un-
federated parts of the world would seem to be this: If the constitutional path had to be avoided for the sake of effective action
even in a federation which already was a working political system,
how much less promising must it be as a starting mode when it is a
matter of bringing together for the first time a number of varied,
and sometimes antagonistic, countries? But if the constitutional
approach, by its very circumspectness, would hold up the start of a
working international system, bold initiative during the period of
emergency at the end of the war might set going lasting instruments and habits of a common international life. And though it
may appear rather brittle, that functional approach would in fact
be more solid and definite than a formal one. It need not meddle
with foundations; old institutions and ways may to some extent
hamper reconstruction, but reconstruction could begin by a common effort without a fight over established ways. Reconstruction
may in this field also prove a surer and less costly way than revolution. As to the new ideologies, since we could not prevent them we
must try to circumvent them, leaving it to the growth of new habits
and interests to dilute them in time. Our aim must be to call forth
to the highest possible degree the active forces and opportunities
for co-operation, while touching as little as possible the latent or
active points of difference and opposition.

There is one other aspect of the post-war period which has been
much discussed and has a bearing on this point, and which helps to
bring out the difference in outlook between the two methods con-
trasted here. Much has been heard of a suggestion that when the
war ends we must have first a period of convalescence and that the
task of permanent reorganization will only come after that. It is a
useful suggestion, insofar as it may help to clear up certain practical problems. But it could also be misleading and even dangerous

if the distinction were taken to justify either putting off the work of international government or differentiating between the agencies by which the new international activities are to be organized, into nurses for convalescence and mentors for the new life. A clean division in time between two such periods in any case is not possible, for the period of convalescence will be different for different activities and ends; but, above all, except for such direct and exceptional consequences of the war as demobilization and the rebuilding of damaged areas, the needs of society will be the same at once after the war as later on. The only difference will be the practical one of a priority of needs, the kind of difference which might be brought about by any social disturbance—an epidemic or an earthquake or an economic crisis—and the urgency of taking action. For the rest, one action and period will merge into the other, according to circumstances. Seed and implements will be as urgent for ensuring the food supply of Europe and Asia as the actual distribution of relief, and indeed more urgent if the war should end after a harvest. Again, both relief and reconstruction will depend greatly on the speedy reorganization and proper use of transport, and so on.

Both circumstances point again to the advantage of a functional practice and to the disadvantage, if not the impossibility, of a comprehensive attempt at political organization. To obtain sufficient agreement for some formal general scheme would, at best, not be possible without delay; at the same time, action for relief and reconstruction will have to start within the hour after the cease-fire. The alternatives would be, if a comprehensive constitutional arrangement is desired and waited for, either to put the immediate work in the hands of temporary international agencies or to leave it to the individual states. The one, in fact, would prepare for the other. Except in matters of relief—the distribution of food, fuel, and clothing and also medical help—*ad hoc* temporary agencies could have no adequate authority or influence; all of what one

might call the society-building activities, involving probably considerable planning and reorganization within and between the several countries, would fall upon the individual states again, as in
1919, when they competed and interfered rather than co-operated
with each other, to the loss of them all. Yet it is vital that international activity should be from the outset in the same hands and
move in the same direction after the war as later; otherwise the
chances of building up an international system would be gravely
prejudiced. It is certain that one of the chief reasons for the failure
of the League was that it was given a formal authority and promissory tasks for the future, while the immediate, urgent, and most
welcome tasks of social reconstruction and reform were left to be
attended to by national agencies. Later efforts to retrieve that mis-
take only led to a series of barren economic conferences, as by that
time the policy of each country was set hard in its own mold. It is
inevitable with any scheme of formal organization that the national
states should have to re-start on their own, and natural therefore
that refuge should be sought in the idea of a period of convalescence while the full-fledged scheme is worked out and adopted. But
functional authorities would not need such political hospitaliza-
tion, with its arbitrary and dangerous division of stages; they
would merely vary, like any other agency anywhere and at any
time, the emphasis of their work in accordance with the changing
condition of their task, continuing to control and organize transport, for instance, after they had rebuilt it, and in the same way
taking each task in hand with a plan and authority for continuing
it. The simple fact is that all the re-starting of agriculture and
industry and transport will either be done on some pre-arranged
common program or it will have to be done, for it could not wait,
on disjointed local plans; it will be done either by pre-established
international agencies or it will have to be done by local national
agencies—and the agencies which will act in the supposed convalescence period will also be those to gather authority and acceptance unto themselves.

Peaceful Change and State Equality in the Functional Order. These are rather general considerations concerning some of the circumstances in which the task will have to begin at the end of the war. When we come to the idea of functional organization itself, it could be argued not only that all *positive* functions could be so organized, but that they might work and develop more freely without constitutional constriction. Admittedly that might prove less easy to justify in regard to the vital *negative* function of law and order. Defense, justice, police, etc., are all instruments of some constituted authority; an international police force, to take the more extreme case, would be an impotent anachronism without an international authority. Yet here again it is true that *ad hoc* functional arrangements have been tried and have worked, where the wider formal unions have been much talked about but not achieved. International policing was effectively tried, under various arrangements, both before and after the First World War. Furthermore, a whole series of functional defense arrangements have been worked out—between Canada, Great Britain, and the United States, between the United States and the states of Latin America —without any changes in their individual or mutual constitutional structure. It is true that these arrangements are related to a state of war; the idea of an American "safety zone" shows how they may evolve into a lasting arrangement of security policing. But let us note especially how these arrangements are bringing into relief the sound lines of a combination of functional and regional organization. The same basis could be applied more effectively than a general one to the judiciary aspects of law and order. The chain of arbitration agreements, the Hague courts, etc., were all in a sense functional arrangements. Perhaps it will be objected that they have not worked; but insofar as they have failed that was not because the method was unworkable, but because the conditions and ends of the pre-war political world were not attuned to the ends and ways of peaceful change.

There is a good way of testing these ideas, in their general nature, by looking at them in the light of two problems which in the traditional systems have had to remain in the realm of theory, but which, because they seem so baffling, may serve to show how solid could be the achievement of a functional order. The first is the pivotal problem of peaceful change. Whether ends justify means or not, certain it is that ends must determine means. Now the method here advocated would be valueless for certain formal changes, and it is therefore necessary to point out that the meaning and purpose of peaceful change have hitherto been greatly confused by an excessive attention to formal issues. As the claimants for revision or changes since the First World War have almost all wanted changes of frontiers, so the reformers in their turn have laid the emphasis on the possible use of Article XIX of the Covenant of the League of Nations to that end. It was easy for more cautious students to show how difficult in fact that would be, and it would be still easier to show that changes of frontiers could not be served by the functional method. But then the functional method by implication denies that there is much international progress to be made through changes of frontiers.[3]

The only sound sense of peaceful change is to do internationally what it does nationally: to make changes of frontiers unnecessary by making frontiers meaningless through the continuous development of common activities and interests across them. A change of frontier is bound to disturb the social life of the groups concerned, no matter whether it comes about peacefully or forcibly. The purpose of peaceful change can only be to prevent such disturbance; one might say indeed that the true task of peaceful change is to remove the need and the wish for changes of frontiers. The functional approach may be justifiably expected to do precisely that: It

[3] See "Territorial Revision and Article 19 of the Covenant," by G. M. Gathorne-Hardy and D. Mitrany, *International Affairs* (London), November-December 1935.

would help the expansion of such positive and constructive common work, of common habits and interests, making frontier lines meaningless by overlaying them with a natural growth of common activities and common administrative agencies. Insofar as it could achieve that result it would also impress a different complexion upon the problem of security. That way alone lies the prospect of turning "defense" into "police," as in the national state; and especially of giving "security" the sense of an undisturbed social life, to be preserved by common government, in lieu of the outdated sense of the security of a physical territory, to be protected by tanks and planes. There is nothing violently new or original about all that. Such a line of action could at most be described in the words applied to the work of Grotius—"an original use of conservative ingredients." Since the turn of the century, especially, international activities have been taken away increasingly from foreign offices and diplomats and placed on a functional basis, and the trend would have achieved much more if its progress had not been obstructed by political division and by war. In many fields arrangements between states have been settled and developed directly in conferences attended by technical experts representing their respective technical departments, without passing through the complicating network of political and diplomatic censors. As a student of this problem put it a few years ago, "The strands of modern international relations spread to every nook and cranny of the governmental machine and weave a pattern as complex as that of domestic administration."

The second problem which may serve as a touchstone is the no less distracting one of state equality. Based as it is on an intractable formal principle, it has in the past caused all efforts at common international action to flounder between the Scylla of power and the Charybdis of sovereignty. On the one side it led the big states to assert their power—as in the Concert of Europe, the Supreme Council at Paris, and the Council of the League; and on the other side the smaller states to flaunt their legal equality—as at the Hague conferences, the League Assembly, and whenever they had an opportunity to bring things to a vote. Innumerable devices have been put forward to try to get around that dilemma. When the Covenant was under discussion the writer proposed a scheme of regional devolution coupled with a hierarchy of representation; the League tried the compromise of adding non-permanent members to the Council, and so on; but these attempts which began as a solution ended as a subterfuge. Hence even in the League the principle of state equality was at best a fiction and at worst the currency of diplomatic bargainings, and in general it has remained a stumbling block in every formal scheme proposed so far. It is worth noting that many a state has also had to face the self-assertion of local groups or provinces or regions—regionalism was a marked phenomenon in the inter-war period—in the face of a growing need for integrated social action. At first sight that may seem paradoxical, but it is natural enough that as the state becomes more highly organized and active, so should the parts, territorial or sectional, become more watchful over their share in the control and benefits of the common organization. That self-interested watchfulness is bound to be even sharper when it is independent states that are to be tied together in some new international formation.

The problem, broadly speaking, is to find an arrangement which would show a measurable and acceptable relation between authority and responsibility, which would exclude no participant arbitrarily from a share in authority, while bringing that share into relation not to sheer power but to the weight of responsibility carried by the several members. The issue is not wholly avoided in a functional organization, but it is sufficiently mitigated to be no longer numbly obstructive, because any transfer of authority would be limited in scope and degree to the purpose in hand. In the democratic countries we would object to giving the executive an all-round increase in power for all time, as a permanent constitutional change, but we are willing to give it all the power it may need for fighting a war or an epidemic, as a limited and specific constitutional increment which could be tested and recalled. In the same way the smaller states have accepted, and indeed invoked, the leadership of the big states in fighting a war or an economic crisis, and there is no reason to believe that they would not also do so in normal times for the sake of a task which all would want to see performed well. Instead of the legal fiction of equality there would thus be an evident and factual inequality in certain spheres, springing from real differences in capacity and interest with regard to some specific function but also limited to that function. It would neither trespass upon fundamental principles nor offend against sentiments of national dignity. Any state can, and usually does, claim in conferences, etc., formal equality with Britain and America. But Rumania is not likely to insist on it if it were a matter of organizing shipping, or Norway if it were a matter of the production of mineral oil; nor would Britain claim it when it came to deal with river pollution and controls on the Continent.

In such cases it is not the state that would be placed in a position of general inferiority, but only a particular service insofar as it was actively inferior. The position of inferiority would be factual and partial, and it would be changeable. A country might rise in the performance of a function and so in the hierarchy of its control; and most countries are likely to have the satisfaction of being in the forefront in some one activity or the other, without regard to their size—like Norway in regard to shipping, Canada in the production of nickel, Rumania in that of oil, Switzerland in international banking, and so on. In any case leadership could be accepted more readily when it rested on evident practical claims and was coupled with practical benefits. As in national affairs, the willingness to grant a measure of power for the sake of good service is likely to temper claims to authority for the sake of prestige. All students and most political spokesmen are insisting that the states must be ready to surrender some of their sovereignty, but is there any prospect that we could secure acceptance for a new view of formal sovereignty, and so of state equality? But the content and working of sovereignty could be modified more effectively by such inconspicuous and partial transfers of authority to international functional organs, just because they would leave untouched a fundamental principle which the smaller states, who are the many, cherish as a bulwark of their independence. The states on the lower Danube made such a transfer to the European Danube Commission and derived benefit from it; they objected only to its being an exceptional arrangement, with a tutelary tinge, and not an international device applied everywhere to similar problems. Insofar as the method becomes general, its political incidence also becomes equal. In other words, that most disruptive and intractable of international principles, the principle of state equality, may well be tamed by specific functional arrangements which would not steal the crown of sovereignty while they would promise something for the purse of necessity.

There would be in this, however, much more than a seemingly underhand change in status. This way could become the path for a gradual progress toward a real equality between nations. If the functional organs would take away something of the formal equality, they would make a substantial return by each contributing something toward a practical equality. In national society also, as in federal states, the way toward social equality is being pursued by pooling resources and equalizing their use—in education and housing, in health and social security, etc.—and that is done generally without any change in constitutional doctrine or political status, though the actual performance is effecting deep changes both in the working of government and in its personnel. Many international problems, like that of the distribution of raw materials and investments, especially that of migration, could not be attacked satisfactorily in any other way. But in that way, through gradual and increasing functional developments, through the provision of common services according to needs, the system would make for that approximation of social conditions and outlook which, better than any constitutional device, might in time build up solid foundations for closer political association.

There is, finally, between states another inequality of which account will have to be taken—not in size or resources, but in political and economic structure. It is an inequality, or rather a dissimilarity which in the inter-war period went deeper than before, as it appears not only in the external form but permeates the whole organization of the state; and it was this that led some advocates of federation to propose a democratic or some such basis for their schemes. We have already suggested that such a criterion would be invidious and unstable; it could in any case not be applied to the group of the United Nations, which range from democratic republics to authoritarian regimes. But if the outward form of the state offers a doubtful guide, either for union or against it, the actual organization of economic and social life presents a real problem if a variety of systems are to be linked up together in their totality. Not all the countries of a possible group have the same organization or interest, and countries with a similar interest are likely to be in various stages of development in that particular respect. There are countries with planned and others with a free economic life; there are industrial countries and agrarian countries. Even if democratic government were postulated for the members of a union, that no longer means laissez faire nowadays. Government controls have everywhere penetrated into economic life, but in varying degrees, which would have to be brought to some common level if the organization is to be formal and comprehensive. Here again it is clear that a formal and comprehensive scheme would imply so much dislocation on the one side and so much adjustment on the other that the difficulties would be almost insuperable, especially in a period of transition and reconstruction already difficult enough in itself; it could certainly not be achieved and made to operate speedily. But functional arrangements could take things as they are and, as far as one can see, could link together specific economic and other activities though in one place they may be in private hands and elsewhere under public control. The electricity grid has done that in England and the TVA in a measure in America. It was done in many a wartime organization. A Danubian Shipping Board would pool and handle all the shipping on the river; how the contribution from each riverain country is organized, and whether its share of profits goes to the state or to private owners, is a matter for that particular country. As a contrast one may recollect how the U.S.S.R. could not participate in the work of the ILO because the latter's constitution called for representation of "employers," in a capitalist sense; whereas if the ILO had simply been empowered to deal with the reality of conditions in, let us say, mining or shipping everywhere, without constitutional prescriptions, its work and influence would have gone straight to the heart of the matter.

The Broad Lines of Functional Organization. The problem of our generation, put very broadly, is how to weld together the common interests of all without interfering unduly with the particular ways of each. It is a parallel problem to that which faces us in national society, and which in both spheres challenges us to find an alternative to the totalitarian pattern. A measure of centralized planning and control, for both production and distribution, is no longer to be avoided, no matter what the form of the state or the doctrine of its constitution. Through all that variety of political forms there is a growing approximation in the working of government, with differences merely of degree and of detail. Liberal democracy needs a re-definition of the public and private spheres of action. But as the line of separation is always shifting under the pressure of fresh social needs and demands, it must be left free to move with those needs and demands and cannot be fixed through a constitutional re-statement. The only possible principle of democratic confirmation is that public action should be undertaken only where and when and insofar as the need for common action becomes evident and is accepted for the sake of the common good. In that way controlled democracy could yet be made the golden mean whereby social needs might be satisfied as largely and justly as possible, while still leaving as wide a residue as possible for the free choice of the individual.

That is fully as true for the international sphere. It is indeed the only way to combine, as well as may be, international organization with national freedom. We have already suggested that not all interests are common to all, and that the common interests do not concern all countries in the same degree. A territorial union would bind together some interests which are not of common concern to the group, while it would inevitably cut asunder some interests of common concern to the group and those outside it. The only way to avoid that twice-arbitrary surgery is to proceed by means of a natural selection, binding together those interests which are common, where they are common, and to the extent to which they are common. That functional selection and organization of international needs would extend, and in a way resume, an international development which has been gathering strength since the latter part of the nineteenth century. The work of organizing international public services and activities was taken a step further by the League, in its health and drug-control work, in its work for refugees, in the experiments with the transfer of minorities and the important innovations of the League loan system, and still more through the whole activity of the ILO. But many other activities and interests in the past had been organized internationally by private agencies—in finance and trade and production, etc., not to speak of scientific and cultural activities. In recent years some of these activities have been brought under public national control in various countries; in totalitarian countries indeed all of them. In a measure, therefore, the present situation represents a retrogression from the recent past: the new turn toward self-sufficiency has spread from economics to the things of the mind; and while flying and wireless were opening up the world, many old links forged by private effort have been forcibly severed. It is unlikely that most of them could be resumed now except through public action, and if they are to operate as freely as they did in private hands they cannot be organized otherwise than on a non-discriminating functional basis.

What would be the broad lines of such a functional organization of international activities? The essential principle is that activities would be selected specifically and organized separately—each according to its nature, to the conditions under which it has to operate, and to the needs of the moment. It would allow, therefore, all freedom for practical variation in the organization of the several functions, as well as in the working of a particular function as needs and conditions alter. Let us take as an example the group of functions which fall under communications, on which the success of post-war reconstruction will depend greatly. What is the proper basis for the international organization of *railway* systems? Clearly it must be European, or rather *continental,* North American, and so on, as that gives the logical administrative limit of co-ordination. A division of the Continent into separate democratic and totalitarian unions would not achieve the practical end, as political division would obstruct that necessary co-ordination; while British and American participation would make the organization more cumbersome without any added profit to the function. As regards shipping, the line of effective organization which at once suggests itself is *international,* or inter-continental, but not universal. A European union could not solve the problem of maritime co-ordination without the co-operation of America and of certain other overseas states. *Aviation* and *broadcasting,* a third example in the same group, could be organized effectively only on a *universal* scale, with perhaps subsidiary regional arrangements for more local services. Such subsidiary regional arrangements could in fact be inserted at any time and at any stage where that might prove useful for any part of a function. Devolution according to need would be as easy and natural as centralization, whereas if the basis of organization were political every such change in dimension would involve an elaborate constitutional re-arrangement. Similarly, it could be left safely to be determined by practical considerations whether at the points where functions cross each other—such as rail and river transport in Europe or civil flying in Europe and America—the two activities should be merely co-ordinated or put under one control.

These are relatively simple examples. The functional co-ordination of production, trade, and distribution evidently would be more complex, especially as they have been built up on a competitive basis. But the experience with international cartels, with the re-organization of the shipping, cotton, and steel industries in England, not to speak of the even wider and more relevant experience with economic co-ordination in the two world wars—all shows that the thing can be done and that it has always been done on such functional lines. No fixed rule is needed, and no rigid pattern is desirable for the organization of these working functional strata.

A certain degree of fixity would not be out of place, however, in regard to more *negative* functions, especially those related to law and order, but also to any others of a more formal nature which are likely to remain fairly static. Security, for instance, could be organized on an interlocking regional basis, and the judicial function likewise, with a hierarchy of courts, as the need may arise—the wider acting as courts of appeal from the more local courts. Yet even in regard to security, and in addition to regional arrangements, the elasticity inherent in functional organization may prove practicable and desirable, if only in the period of transi-

tion. Anglo-American naval co-operation for the policing of the
seas may prove acceptable for a time, and it would cut across
physical regions. Agreement on a mineral sanction would of necessity mean common action by those countries which control the
main sources; and other such combinations might be found useful
for any particular task in hand. That is security only for defense;
security arrangements were conceived usually on a geographical
basis because they were meant to prevent violence, and that would
still be the task of sanctions, etc., based on some regional devolution. But in addition there is a growing functional devolution in the
field of social security in connection with health, with the drug and
white slave traffic, with crime, etc. In all that important field of
social policing it has been found that co-ordination and co-operation with the police of other countries on functional lines, varying
with each task, was both indispensable and practicable. There is
no talk and no attempt in all this to encroach upon sovereignty,
but only a detached functional association which works smoothly
and is already accepted without question.

However that may be, in the field of more *positive* active functions—economic, social, cultural—which are varied and ever
changing in structure and purpose, any devolution must, like the
main organization, follow functional lines. Land transport on the
Continent would need a different organization and agencies should
the railways after a time be displaced by roads; and a Channel
tunnel would draw England into an arrangement in which she does
not at present belong, with a corresponding change in the governing organ.

Here we discover a cardinal virtue of the functional method—
what one might call the virtue of technical self-determination. The
functional *dimensions,* as we have seen, determine themselves. In a
like manner the function determines its appropriate *organs.* It also
reveals through practice the nature of the action required under the
given conditions, and in that way the *powers* needed by the respec-

tive authority. The function, one might say, determines the executive instrument suitable for its proper activity, and by the same process provides a need for the reform of the instrument at every stage. This would allow the widest latitude for variation between functions, and also in the dimension or organization of the same function as needs and conditions change. Not only is there in all this no need for any fixed constitutional division of authority and power, prescribed in advance, but anything beyond the original formal definition of scope and purpose might embarrass the working of the practical arrangements.

The Question of Wider Co-ordination. The question will be asked, however, in what manner and to what degree the various functional agencies that may thus grow up would have to be linked to each other and articulated as parts of a more comprehensive organization. It should be clear that each agency could work by itself, but that does not exclude the possibility of some of them or all being bound in some way together, if it should be found needful or useful to do so. That indeed is the test. As the whole sense of this particular method is to let activities be organized as the need for joint action arises and is accepted, it would be out of place to lay down in advance some formal plan for the co-ordination of various functions. Co-ordination, too, would in that sense have to come about functionally. Yet certain needs and possibilities can be foreseen already now, though some are probable and others only likely, and it may help to round off the picture if we look into this aspect briefly.

1. *Within the same group* of functions probably there would have to be co-ordination either simply for technical purposes or for wider functional ends, and this would be the first stage toward a wider integration. To take again the group concerned with communications—rail, road, and air transport in Europe would need *technical* co-ordination in regard to timetables, connections, etc. They may need also a wider *functional* co-ordination if there is to

be some distribution of passenger and freight traffic for the most economic performance—whether that is done by a superior executive agency or by some arbitral body, perhaps on the lines of the Federal Commerce Commission in America. Sea and air traffic across the Atlantic or elsewhere, though separately organized, probably would also benefit from a similar type of co-ordination. Again, various mineral controls, if they should be organized separately, would need some co-ordination, though this arbitrary grouping of "minerals" would be less to the point than the co-ordination of specific minerals and other products with possible substitutes—of crude oil with synthetic oil, of crude rubber with synthetic rubber, and so on.

2. The next degree or stage might be, if found desirable, the co-ordination of *several groups* of functional agencies. For instance, the communications agencies may not only work out some means of acting together in the distribution of orders for rolling stock, ships, etc., but they could or should work in this through any agencies that may have come into being for controlling materials and production, or through some intermediary agency as a clearinghouse. There is no need to prescribe any pattern in advance, or that the pattern adopted in one case should be followed in all the others.

3. The co-ordination of such working functional agencies with any *international planning* agencies would present a third stage, and one that brings out some interesting possibilities, should the ideas for an international investment board or an international development commission, as an advisory organ, come to fruition. One can see how such a development commission might help to guide the growth of functional agencies into the most desirable channels, and could watch their inter-relations and their repercussions. And an investment board could guide, for instance, the distribution of orders for ships, materials, etc., not only according to the best economic use but also for the purpose of ironing out

cyclical trends. It could use, according to its nature, its authority or its influence to make of such orders a means additional to international public works, etc., for dealing with periods or pockets of unemployment. Co-ordination of such a general kind may in some cases amount almost to arbitration of differences between functional agencies; regional boards or councils like those of the Pan-American Union might be used to adjust or arbitrate regional differences.

4. Beyond this there remains the habitual assumption, as we have already said, that international action must have some overall *political authority* above it. Besides the fact that such a comprehensive authority is not now a practical possibility, it is the central view of the functional approach that such an authority is not essential for our greatest and real immediate needs. The several functions could be organized through the agreement, given specifically in each case, of the national governments chiefly interested, with the grant of the requisite powers and resources; whereas it is clear, to emphasize the previous point, that they could not allow such organizations simply to be prescribed by some universal authority, even if it existed. For an authority which had the title to do so would in effect be hardly less than a world government; and such a strong central organism would inevitably tend to take unto itself rather more authority than that originally allotted to it, this calling in turn for the checks and balances which are used in federal systems, but which would be difficult to provide in any loose way. If issues should arise in any functional system which would call either for some new departure or for the re-consideration of existing arrangements, that could be done only in council by all the governments concerned. Insofar as it may be desired to keep alive some general view of our problems, and perhaps a general watch over the policies of the several joint agencies, some body of a representative kind, like the League Assembly or the governing body of the ILO, could meet periodically, perhaps

elected by proportional representation from the assemblies of the member states. Such an assembly, in which all the states would have a voice, could discuss and ventilate general policies, as an expression of the mind and will of public opinion; but it could not actually prescribe policy, as this might turn out to be at odds with the policy of governments. Any line of action recommended by such an assembly would have to be pressed and secured through the policy-making machinery of the various countries themselves.

These, then, are the several types and grades of co-ordination which might develop with the growth of functional activities. But there is, finally, in the political field also the problem of security, admittedly a crucial problem, for on its being solved effectively the successful working of the other activities will depend. At the same time, the general discussion of functional organization will have served to bring out the true place and proportion of security, as something indispensable but also as something incapable by itself of achieving the peaceful growth of an international society. It is in fact a separate function like the others, not something that stands in stern isolation, overriding all the others. Looking at it in this way, as a practical function, should also make it clear that we would not achieve much if we handled it as a one-sided, limited problem—at present too often summed up in "German aggression." German aggression was a particularly vicious outgrowth of a bad general system, and only a radical and general change of the system itself will provide continuous security for all. In this case also it would be useful to lay down some formal pledges and principles as a guiding line, but the practical organization would have to follow functional, perhaps combined with regional, lines. That is all the more necessary as we know better now how many elements besides the purely military enter into the making of security. The various functional agencies might, in fact, play an important role in that wider aspect of security; they could both watch over and check such things as the building of strategic railways or the accumulation of strategic stocks in metals or grains. Possibly they could even be used, very properly and effectively, as a first line of action against threatening aggression, by their withholding services from those who are causing the trouble. They could apply such preventive sanctions more effectively than if this were to wait upon the agreement and action of a number of separate governments; and they could do so as part of their practical duties, and therefore with less of the political reactions caused by political action.

Representation in Controls. One aspect likely to be closely examined is that of the structure of the functional controls, and here again the initial difficulty will be that we shall have to break away from attractive traditional ideas if we are to work out the issue on its merits. It is not in the nature of the method that representation on the controlling bodies should be democratic in a political sense, full and equal for all. Ideally it may seem that all functions should be organized on a worldwide scale and that all states should have a voice in control. Yet the weight of reality is on the side of making the jurisdiction of the various agencies no wider than the most effective working limits of the function; and while it is understandable that all countries might wish to have a voice in control, that would be really to hark back to the outlook of political sovereignty. In no functional organization so far have the parties interested had a share in control as "by right" of their separate existence—neither the various local authorities in the London Transport Board, nor the seven states concerned in the TVA. And in any case, in the transition from power politics to a functional order we could be well satisfied if the control of the new international organs answered to some of the merits of each case, leaving it to experience and to the maturing of a new outlook to provide in time the necessary correctives.

The new method would have in this regard certain very solid merits: (1) Any claim to a share in control would have to be

justified by a corresponding and evident capacity for performance.
(2) By that test smaller states could also qualify and the participants in control would vary, thus avoiding an excessive accumulation of influence in the hands of a few countries. (3) The same test
again would in each case govern not only the fact of participation
in control, but also the extent of the powers of control. (4) The
performance would be practical and measurable, with a periodical
balance sheet (more definite and more suitable for examination
than, e.g., the reports to the League's Mandates Commission),
through which the work and the policy of each agency could be
closely checked. Czechs and Swiss may possibly dislike not having
a direct part in the control of an international shipping board, and
it is true that as consumers they would run a certain risk, as with
such a monopolistic board they could not drive the bargains that
are possible when shipping is run by a number of competing private undertakings. Yet in this case also they would have no direct
voice in control, and would be equally powerless against a shipping
cartel; whereas the organization of shipping as a recognized common service would give them a standing in court, so to speak, with
a right to bring open plaint for any particular grievances and even
to criticize on general grounds any failings of the service. To this
might be added that from all past experience a personnel which
would be largely technical and permanent is likely to develop both
a professional pride and a vested interest in good performance.
That is an important point, and one that helps to bring out in this
case, too, how formal ideas of equality may actually stand in the
way of practical achievement. For "equal representation" involves
not only the presence but also the character of representation; it is
not merely a matter of being represented but clearly of being
represented by people of one's own choice who will express one's
particular interests. The demand for equal share in control is only
too likely to lead to that for an equal or proportional share in
personnel, and that would be to build up within the various agen-

cies a mass of national groups rather than a detached international civil service. Yet the growth of such a service would be the best insurance against any possible abuse; just as the functional method itself, by concentrating all attention on a practical common service, is likely more than anything else to breed a new conscience in all those concerned with such international activities.

This line of action would help to develop also another factor that is needed for the good working of any such experiment— namely, an international outlook and public opinion. The very fact that it would concentrate attention on practical issues and activities would give people a better chance than the habitual political arguments to judge it on its merits. And as it would be natural to vary the seat of the various agencies, placing it in each case at a convenient center for the particular function, people in many parts of the world would have before their eyes a piece of international government in action.

It must be expected that the idea of an equal voice and the demand for it will die hard, in spite of its hollowness in all past experience, and that the ideas accepted here will appear to some as a surrender to power. Power, unfortunately, is one of the facts of international life that have to be reckoned with, but it would be a great step forward to harness it to a common task, for common ends, and in a measure under common control. In that way the less powerful and less wealthy peoples would at least get some of the reality of equality, for limitation in executive control does not imply exclusion from participation in the work and in its benefits, or indeed in the shaping of more general lines of policy. If, for instance, the main suppliers of capital might have to have a leading role in an international investment board, which would be an executive agency, all the countries could and should be represented on an eventual international development commission, which would debate and recommend in an advisory capacity the general line of economic action. That kind of inequality is inevitable when the contributions will be so unequal and while the method is still on trial, though one might hope that gradually the functional agencies would acquire a purely technical form of management, based no longer even on contributions but on the capacity of the managers for their jobs; it would be, one might say, equality in non-representation. But to insist on rearing a system from the outset on the legal principle of equality could only lead to one of two things: Either any effective action would be blocked again—for how far would the Great Powers be likely to go in allowing their capital and resources and so on to be disposed of by majority decisions? —or, if they agreed among themselves, the big states would probably feel impelled to take matters into their own hands. Can anyone doubt that these are the inescapable alternatives? Already amidst renewed professions about the equality of nations one hears increasingly the theme of the responsibility of the Great Powers for shaping the world to come, and with it murmurs of incipient revolt among the smaller states against that assumption of a "rich man's burden." Just as the elusiveness of the traditional political approach led those who cling to it to seek the respite of a "convalescence period," so its contradictions lead them either to try to shift responsibility for the future upon some vague European or other council, or to fall back in baffled exasperation upon the special claims and standing of the four allied Powers.[4] That is the dilemma

---

[4] When these pages were written there was already a division of outlook on this issue. The Big Four were asserting their special claims and responsibility, while the smaller states, including neutrals, were showing open resentment at that arbitrary self-assertion. In the form which it took the attitude of the leading Allies was a sheer assertion of power, without any open and practical examination of the needs and tasks before us; and for that reason at the first real test it collapsed, bringing down with it the important plan for a joint United Nations Relief and Rehabilitation Administration.

Its original draft constitution was an intelligent and probably effective compromise between power in the central council, equality in the regional councils, and technical autonomy in the executive body; and its scope was to be far-reaching. But as far as one can see, the whole conception was scuttled at the Atlantic City Conference (November 1943), when the

to which the idea of formal equality leads inexorably: equality without government, or government without equality. But this kind of inequality would be political and arbitrary and therefore less controllable in its ends and in its means; hence we must have the ingenuity and detachment to devise a more satisfactory adjustment between the principle of legal equality and the needs of a working equality.

Through Functional Action to International Society

The Way of Natural Selection. One cannot insist too much that such gradual functional developments would not create a new system, however strange they might appear in the light of our habitual search for a unified formal order. They would merely rationalize and develop what is already there. In all countries social activities, in the widest sense of the term, are organized

---

smaller states successfully asserted their sovereign equality and the Big Four readily assented to it. First the chief task of joint action, co-ordinated reconstruction, was given up and the scope of U.N.R.R.A. whittled down to relief; and then all action beyond the procurement of supplies was put back into the hands of individual governments. Even the elementary proposal that the inland transport of supplies in Europe should be put under some joint authority was thwarted. No one who knows the state of Europe could doubt that this put all reconstruction in jeopardy, both politically and socially. It meant in the first place that the life of Europe was abandoned again to nationalist competition, against which an anemic U.N.R.R.A. would not long survive. It meant also that instead of being used to satisfy the new social trends, in the hands of the ruling groups economic resources would be used in an effort to retain political control. Having based their own claims on power, the Big Four, or rather Three, were thus led to give power a free rein everywhere. On that basis any international organization would be little more than a façade. That miscarriage shows how futile was the hope of those who thought of getting through federation or such political schemes a deliberate surrender of sovereignty; as it brings out the desperate need of securing before the end of the war practical arrangements for common international action. This would be a much truer test of the will for international peace than any vaguely promissory charter or covenant.

and reorganized continually in that way. But because of the legalistic structure of the state and of our political outlook, which
treat national and international society as two different worlds,
social nature, so to speak, has not had a chance so far to take its
course. Our social activities are cut off arbitrarily at the limit of the
state and, if at all, are allowed to be linked to the same activities
across the border only by means of uncertain and cramping political
ligatures. What is here proposed is simply that these political am-
putations should cease. Whenever useful or necessary the several
activities would be released to function as one unit throughout the
length of their natural course. National problems would then appear, and would be treated, as what they are—the local segments
of general problems. There is a lesson to be drawn from the fact
that federal states, even more than unitary states, do of necessity
develop their common life on a functional basis. In Australia, in
the face of a fairly rigid constitution, as new problems come up
there is ever more experimenting with extra-constitutional machinery. Because the states could not raise foreign loans in competition, nor would readily submit to federal control, they have built
up a Loan Council for use by the federation as well as by the
states. When several experiments with marketing schemes were
invalidated on constitutional grounds other roundabout schemes
had to be worked out by negotiation, and the Tariff Board provides yet another example of the application of the functional
principle. As many illustrations could be given from Canada, and
many more from the United States under the New Deal. In America it would have been utterly impossible to reconstruct the federal
authority through constitutional changes, but by a gradual accumulation of new functional tasks and powers the government at
Washington now has come to represent a working unity which has
welded the life of the country together more solidly than the Constitution ever did or could. In his *Survey of American Foreign
Relations*, 1928, the late Mr. Charles Howland listed this prefer-

ence for specific action as one of the four fundamental American traditions; while suspicious of "entangling alliances," this was the type of international action which America had always favored and never feared.

Such examples which show how the functional trend is making headway under federal constitutions also go to show that in the international field too such functional beginnings could grow in time into a rounded political system. There is nothing incompatible between the two conceptions; the functional arrangements might indeed be regarded as organic elements of a federalism by installments. But such a federalism, if it came, would be the solid growth of a natural selection and evolution, tested and accepted by experience, and not a green-table creation blown about and battered by all the winds of political life. A functional organization does not crack if one of the participants tries political or social experiments of his own. Nor indeed would its existence be in jeopardy, as would be that of a sectional federation, if one of the members were to secede altogether. If the seceding member or members should happen to be pivotal factors in certain activities the result might be serious, but even then only the particular function affected would be endangered, while the others could go on. Or a state could drop out of certain functions but continue in others, as Japan continued to share in the work of the ILO after she resigned from the League. Some participants could drop out, that is, or some functions could be abandoned without wrecking the system as a whole. Contrariwise, a function could be resumed, or a member might return, without political upheaval. In the past, indeed, after international wars, proved functional arrangements have often been resumed as a matter of course, in spite of passions roused and frontiers changed. Constitutional arrangements would inevitably be shaken in the former cases and altogether broken in the latter case.

Politically the method would have the strength which comes

from free growth. No country need be forced to come in, and no country would be forced to stay out. Countries would come in for those functional activities in which they would be entitled to participate by the weight of their interests and resources, but all countries would benefit from the performance of a general service, even if they had no part in its control. On the other hand, no one would share in power who did not share in responsibility. This good democratic postulate could be reinforced by democratic representation; the functional structure could be made a real union of peoples, not of states, but of the people directly concerned in any specific function, by giving them functional representation somewhat on the lines of the governing organ of the ILO.

The future lies clearly with a more liberal and systematic development on these lines. Not all activities can or need be so organized. But in all essential activities we could advance from our present position effectively and without delay if we would but put out of our minds the old political argument between political centralism and political devolution, which was the concomitant of the passive liberal state, and follow a line more closely fitting the actual progress of our communal life. Instead of breaking up government mechanically into a pyramid of subordinate territorial areas, we need for our new ends rather to dissect its tasks and relevant authorities on lines that correspond to and fit those tasks. Instead of keeping up the old and barren attempt to establish a formal and fixed division of sovereignty and power, a division which changing conditions continually puts out of joint, we could with a little insight and boldness distribute power in accordance with the practical requirements of every function and object. Instead, that is, of asking *by whom* should sovereignty and power be exercised, we should rather ask *upon what* objects they should be exercised; or to put it in other words, the real question is not "Who are the rightful authorities?" but rather "What are the rightful ends—and what the proper means for them?" Authority would derive from the performance of a common task and would be conditioned by it, and not from the possession of a separate "right." Once we accept the idea of the functional organization of government, those instances will become self-evident in which the regional or worldwide extension of the service and of the attendant power would be demanded by the obvious needs of the case, and could not be refused on grounds of existing political separation without doing evident violence to the needs of the governed and to the very meaning of government. Such spontaneous growths as those to which we have briefly referred prove that there are certain branches of public affairs not local or national but affecting the whole part of the world over which they stretch. They are, so to speak, not *areas* but *strata* of government, varying like geological strata in their expanse; and they cannot be effectively dealt with except as such, in the interest both of the performance and of the people whom it concerns, and not least in the interest of the peaceful flow of international relations.

Some Wartime Experiences. The needs of the war have brought about some actual experiments on the lines discussed, and these experiments have worked well in practice. A whole series of joint agencies has grown up, greatly varying in structure and purpose, and that very variety shows how necessary it was found to build the organization around the job. None of these agencies was conceived theoretically in advance, but each was set up in answer to a proved need. No form was prescribed in advance, to conform to some habitual pattern, but each task was given an appropriate organization, and the organization was allowed to adapt and re-form itself in the light of experience. The same pragmatic approach was allowed to rule the measures for the co-ordination of various activities and agencies. Finally, and most striking of all— though in some cases, especially between America and Canada, the arrangements went very far indeed, affecting each country's domestic policy—it was never attempted or suggested that they should be put upon a political-constitutional basis. Everybody knew indeed that these functional arrangements would have been difficult to bring about if they had implied, as a necessity, such constitutional adjustments. Almost everything that has been done illustrates both sides of that political aspect—how the specific functional activities were set in motion and worked effectively without political attachments and how, in some cases at any rate, the dislike of political attachments actually hindered the growth of joint practical activities.

A number of international agencies existed already before the war. There were, for example, the International Union of Railways and the International Railway Congress, the League of Nations' International Transit Committee, and the International Transport Office of the Berne Convention; the postal services had the Postal Union and the Union Télégraphique Universelle, to which might be added the Union Internationale de Radio-Diffusion. There was a World Power conference and a Standards Committee, and also a Latin monetary union, though this had broken down under the stress of inflation during the First World War. Most of these were, however, only embryonic functional agencies, for the periodical co-ordination of separate national services and policies. The agencies which have grown up during the Second World War go much further and are possessed of delegated executive power. It would be out of place to attempt to give here a list of these various executive bodies, but they illustrate almost every type, both in the scope of their activities and in the range of their jurisdiction. As regards participation, they vary from many two-sided arrangements between Great Britain and America, and Canada and America, to those in which several of the United Nations are included, always on the basis of their special interest in the particular function. Limitation in formal participation does not, of course, imply limitation in service. The Anglo-American Raw Materials Board, for instance, was instructed from the outset to collaborate also with the other United Nations for the most effective use of their joint resources. "As a result of the Board's activities," says the official report on the first year of operation, "world traffic in raw materials among the United Nations now flows in orderly fashion. The Board provides a meeting ground where all can go and get a decision—a decision that will be accepted and implemented." A somewhat different basis of representation was adopted when the action contemplated was meant to embrace a definite region: the Middle East Supply Center and the economic work of the Pan-American Union illustrate such regional action, though they differ greatly from one another. In neither case was regional co-ordination exclusive in character; whatever measures were taken there to further regional development in no way precluded their being linked up also with wider international action in the same fields.

One indirect result of the establishment of the Raw Materials Board well illustrates how functional action generates in a natural way whatever machinery it needs. For the international work which is its proper function the Board has to keep in regular contact with a number of departments in each participating state, and this has led to a measure of national co-ordination which did not otherwise exist in the respective countries. The Board has set up to that end an Advisory Operating Committee on which are represented, from the U.S., the State Department, the War Production Board, the Department of Commerce, and the Board of Economic Warfare; and from the United Kingdom, the Foreign Office, the Ministry of Production, the Ministry of Supply, and the Ministry of Economic Warfare. International co-ordination had thus brought out the need for national co-ordination in the particular field, and also produced the necessary machinery.

The same adaptable variety is to be found in the activity of other war agencies. Some of them, as their names imply, are concerned with a single product or service; others, like the Raw Materials Board, control a number of products. Again, there is the

American-Canadian agreement of April 1942, under which the
two countries have adopted a mutual division of labor for certain
farm products and also facilities for the better mutual use of agricultural machinery and seasonal labor, and without any changes in
the structure of their tariffs. To these might be added the joint
American-Canadian economic committee which is studying post-
war collaboration in the region tapped by the new Alaska Highway
—itself built as a joint enterprise. It has been suggested that for
economic purposes, and possibly in the matter of administration,
the development of that area of about one million square miles
should go as a joint undertaking of the two countries, without
regard to national boundary lines. The various proposals for a
Danubian TVA imply a similar idea in which, however, a larger
number of countries would be involved.

A typical instance of the free growth of which such specific
agencies are capable is offered by the Middle East Supply Center,
in the matter both of its growth and of its organization. The center
was set up to review the joint resources and civilian needs of the
Middle East, so as to make the area as self-supporting as it could
be. Its first task was to work out a shipping program as far ahead
as possible, and this led it progressively to discuss with the local
governments the priority of their needs, how to increase production and improve distribution; and upon that basis it advised the
authorities responsible for shipping and outside supplies. Its jurisdiction covered at first the countries around the Eastern Mediter-
ranean and the Red Sea, but later it was extended to include Iraq,
Persia, and Saudi Arabia; and while at first it was organized as a
British Agency, it became a combined British and American agency
in 1942.

These repeated adaptations would have been difficult if the Center had been set up on the basis of some formal treaty or pact. It is
true that the arrangement was also made easier by its being made
as a war measure on the war authority of England and America.

For any long-term purpose the countries of the Middle East would have to be given a more real share in control, and this already is the trend. In 1943, conferences in which their governments took part were held on road transport, the anti-locust campaign, food control and rationing, and statistical information. Collaboration in such matters, to which agricultural policy should be added, must bind the Arab countries closer together; whereas a mainly political approach would be less solid and would render suspect any idea of collaboration with countries outside the region. The same fear of political intrusion under cover of economic co-operation has undoubtedly slowed down the otherwise great possibilities of Pan-American regional developments. Where there are no such fears, the functional arrangements have grown freely in spite of different political ties. Functional links between Canada and America, and even between England and America, have grown faster and closer than within the British Empire. The Empire has only a loose co-ordinating body, the Commonwealth Supply Council, and it is significant, if somewhat curious, that Canada is not represented on it.

The general trend of these war experiments has been summarized by an American scholar as follows: "The lines between domestic and international activity are blurred, and national administrative agencies of the Powers concerned sometimes engage in domestic business, and at other times extend their functions into the international sphere. The result is a conglomeration of international boards and domestic staffs, whose duties intermingle. Administrative officers of national units deal directly with their opposite numbers in other states without benefit of diplomatic intermediaries, and simultaneously perform both national and international tasks. So far no attempt has been made to establish a super-state."[5]

[5] J. Payson Wild, Jr., *Machinery of Collaboration between the United Nations.* Foreign Policy Association Report, July 1, 1942.

The contrast is supplied by the two attempts to start organizing eastern Europe on federal lines. The first steps for Polish-Czecho-slovak and for Greek-Yugoslav union, taken by the respective governments under friendly pressure from well-intentioned but ill-advised Western allies, have proved worse than abortive; they have come to nothing, and have hardened the feeling that nothing can be done in that region. Another negative example, in a secondary field, was the attempt of the British Trade Union Congress to build up closer relations with American labor. Because only one trade union group in each country could be affiliated with the International Federation of Trade Unions, the T.U.C. proceeded constitutionally and attempted to work through the American Federation of Labor alone; that inevitably got it into difficulties with the other American group, the new and more influential Congress of Industrial Organizations. In the end not only did the English move fail, it also added a further element of dissension between the two rival American groups. But if the T.U.C., in the face of that division, had made its approach on a functional tack—from miners to miners, from engineers to engineers, and so on—it might have been able to work around the constitutional obstacle and to build up a solid, if more gradual, connection with the whole of American labor.[6]

The Tasks Ahead. In a statement given out with the first annual report of the Combined Raw Materials Board, Mr. Batt, its American member, pointed out that serious as was the raw mate-

[6] One is tempted to apply these lessons to another type of case, that of India, though this is, of course, mere speculation. The attempt to work toward Indian independence along constitutional federal lines actually deepened and hardened the division between Moslems and Hindus. But it is at least arguable that if the Indian demand for self-government had been met through a series of functional transfers of authority, covering in each case the whole country, that approach might have given India, with growing autonomy, also a growing unity, while it would have touched as little as possible the intractable religious-political issue.

rials problem during the war, it could become worse in the postwar period. At present there were only a limited number of purchasers and a limited shipping capacity to carry what was available, but after the war there was likely to be a scramble by all the nations to lay hands on supplies. "Experience after the First World War," said Mr. Batt, " has shown that such a scramble can result in complete demoralization of supply, price, and other factors in peacetime economy. It is impossible to see how such a situation can be met unless there is some form of combined machinery." The dangers which might threaten international reconstruction in this respect are twofold: first, the kind of competition of which Mr. Batt spoke and, second, the adoption everywhere of national economic plans without any corresponding international adjustments. In February 1943, for instance, the Royal Agricultural Society of England recommended the setting up after the war of a statutory body, on the lines of the Forestry Commission, to deal with food production and control in all their aspects. Such a national functional body could do a great deal of good, but unless it were linked to some international program and organization the very desire to bring in this field order at home may lead to disorder abroad; and then all the fine social ideas for ensuring "freedom from want" may be mangled in the ruthless maw of international competition. These twin dangers, closely connected, have been starkly illuminated by recent discussions in England and in America on the future of civil aviation. Private interests have not unnaturally felt that they must stake out their claims in good time, and they have been using the customary arguments of national interest and safety and honor.[7] The problem of international avia-

[7] Mr. A. N. Kemp, president of American Airlines, Inc.: "Our air efforts must not relax with victory. Immediate development and expansion of America's aviation is necessary to protect our nation at the peace conference. Then, either we will be dominant in the air—or we will be dominated in the post-war air world." (*Daily Telegraph,* February 11.) Mr. Theodore Instone: "Unless Britain, with the British Commonwealth, has parity in the

tion is indeed especially dangerous just because of the fears which
it might harbor, or which it might serve to rouse. It touches, as the
Manchester Guardian wrote (March 13, 1943), "all the sensitive
spots" of the post-war situation, "and is one of the most far-reaching of all the tests of our capacity for co-operation." To which *The
Times* added the crucial point that—both because air transport is
bound to be in a large measure international transport and because
past experience has shown that issues of civil aviation cannot be
well separated from issues of military aviation which vitally affect
international security—little progress can be made toward solving
the problems of air transport "in any one country pending a settlement of the major issue of international organization throughout
the world."

The task that is facing us is how to build up the reality of a
common interest in peace. But with a revolutionary element injected into war that demands also a new sense of peace: not a
peace that would keep the nations quietly apart but a peace that
would bring them actively together, not the old static and strategic
view but a social view of peace. Or one might say that we
must put our faith not in a protected peace but in a working peace;
it would indeed be nothing more nor less than the idea and aspiration of social security taken in its widest range. The number of
problems which take on a world character is growing apace, partly

---

air with any other nation she will cease to be a great power." (*Daily Telegraph,* March 4.) Mr. Walter Runciman: "We must see that there is an
area in Europe quite as free as the United States, and without rival aircraft factories competing with one another. You have got to get them to
use the best aircraft produced in the entire Continent . . . if you are not
going to have the Americans overrunning the whole of the European
routes." (*The Times,* March 10.) The Joint Air Transport Committee
(representing the Association of British Chambers of Commerce, the
Federation of British Industries, and the London Chamber of Commerce):
"Freedom of the Air" is an issue that "vitally affects the future greatness of
Britain and the Empire. It is certainly not a nostrum to be included without
thought among the freedoms for which we fight." (*The Times,* March 11.)

because we have a better understanding of them—and know that with economics, as with epidemics and drugs, the evil must be attacked at the source and therefore through international action —but also because of their technical peculiarities. Such is the nature of all the wonderful new technical inventions that each harbors within it as much a threat as a promise. That was so with the steamship and still more with the submarine; and while flying and wireless bring comforts, they also bring fears. One threatens to interfere with the domestic safety of all people, and the other with their domestic sentiments and peace of mind. And airplanes and broadcasts cannot simply be denied access by a sovereign authority as was possible with ships and trains and telegraph; they drop upon us literally from the skies. Hence these new contacts which crowd upon us from all directions can be as much a source of conflict as of co-operation; they must be built up in friendship for common use, or they will grow foul around us in suspicion and competition.

Empire and League having failed to find a way to an active international unity, because outstripped in different ways by the growth of social life, some reformers would now try federation; yet the very number and variety of the schemes proposed, limited territorially or ideologically, show that a scheme that might bring all peoples together cannot even be thought of. Federation, like other political formations, carries a Janus head which frowns division on one side in the very act of smiling union on the other. The idea which would look upon the United Nations as the grouping of the future is more spacious but less solid; it would break up the world upon no sounder basis than the chance alliance of war, and such a miscellaneous grouping on the basis of political equality would hardly suit the needs of executive action in the great tasks ahead. The growth of new administrative devices, and especially of planned public action, must be followed up also in the international sphere if the latter is to be more than a shadow. The organization of all social activities on a universal scale and on such lines is not yet practicable. Federal schemes, though they take account of the new factor, are logical only on a limited scale, at the expense of general unity. There remains the functional method. It is by no means free of difficulties, but on the whole these are mechanical difficulties which one could hope to overcome, and not political difficulties that spring from the very act of creation of the new organization.

Moreover, if a closer union was not found necessary, and probably would not have been accepted, even in the dire straits of war, what reason is there to think that it will be more acceptable when the victorious countries will be standing on their own feet again? But it is worth noting, on the other hand, that in times of stress the nations always adopt certain types of government, the shape and working of which are dictated by the task and by the conditions in which it is performed. Already in the First World War the two groups of belligerents, though they had no intercourse with one another and varied greatly in political structure and outlook, were found afterward to have used strikingly similar administrative devices to deal with the unforeseen problems of the new war of material attrition. That is largely true in the Second World War also, and the conclusion can only be that in such emergencies government has to be allowed to take a natural course, both in the several countries and in any joint action between them; whereas in normal times, when we face no great risk, we tend to force it into shapes set by dogma and tradition.

As long as these hardy imponderables have such a hold on our political outlook there is no prospect that under a democratic order we could induce the individual states to accept a permanent limitation of their economic sovereignty, by an international authority operating over the whole field; and that is the less likely, as we said at the beginning, at a time when the individual nations are themselves planning anew their own use of it. But while that sifting process is still going on, the nations may well be found willing, as part of their new plans, to transfer strictly limited parts of that sovereignty to international executive agencies entrusted with specific and carefully defined activities; they may accept even general advice and guidance when they would reject any general command. It is not without significance that of the League of Nations only the functional services have survived, including the ILO, and that they are readily assumed to be capable still of playing an active part in any future international scheme. Pivotal countries like the United States and the U.S.S.R. could become vital links in a functional network when they could not all be made parts of any formal political scheme. Nor does it seem possible in any other way to combine national autonomy with universality; national agencies would not be displaced, but might indeed derive fresh life and scope from wide functional co-ordination with the outside world. At the same time, action through functional agencies would check the intrusion of power politics in the guise of foreign help, or the wasteful use of international help by national agencies. Finally, alone in this way could we hope to prevent the damage done to international relations in every so-called peace settlement that prolongs the division into enemies and friends after the conflict. Even if at the end of the war certain disabilities are to be imposed upon our present opponents in the political and military spheres, we could for the rest let them share in those activities which in our interest as much as in theirs need to be organized in common from the outset. That would help all Europe better than reparations, while through such detached co-operation for specific practical ends the peoples whom we now fight would also best be "re-educated" into a new sense of common values. We could do all that without doing violence to our feelings, but also without damaging the world's new life.

There is hope in this also for the growth of what is now well called social security. As General Smuts said in a recent speech,

"This is the social century." Every new international service would bring its contribution to the achievement of freedom from want and fear, and in opening up wide these channels of social action we would also broaden the area of free choice for the common man. Indeed, it is a question whether this might not be the real way to ensure also his other more personal freedoms. The issue goes rather beyond the scope of these pages, but we know from experience that minorities' treaties and declarations of the rights of man, good as it is to have them as assertions of principle, are of little use as instruments of government. They cannot really be enforced by international action. International action could have some influence on the texts of written constitutions but cannot watch the nature and working of administrative law—and administrative laws and agencies are now increasingly the means of government action and, it will be found, also the means by which minorities of whatever kind can now be discriminated against in a less blatant way. For that very reason the growth of international functional agencies should prove a more effective antidote; they could protect the freedom of individuals and minorities in various active sectors of their social life, either directly if in their employment or through administrative agreements with national agencies —as seamen, for instance, through an international shipping agency, and in general as workers or migrants or radio listeners. Here again the simple arithmetic of such specific practical actions may in the end build more solidly than the vast philosophy of general declarations.

Epilogue. Peace will not be secured if we organize the world by what divides it. But in the measure in which such peace-building activities develop and succeed, one might hope that the mere prevention of conflict, crucial as that may be, would in time fall to a subordinate place in the scheme of international things, while we would turn to what are the real tasks of our common society—the conquest of poverty and of disease and of ignorance. The stays of

political federation were needed when life was more local and international activities still loose. But now our social interdependence is all-pervasive and all-embracing, and if it be so organized the political side will also grow as part of it. The elements of a
functional system could begin to work without a general political
authority, but a political authority without active social functions
would remain an empty temple. Society will develop by our living
it, not by policing it. Nor would any political agreement survive
long under economic competition, but economic unification would
build up the foundation for political agreement, even if it did not
make it superfluous. In any case, as things are, the political way is
too ambitious. We cannot start from an ideal plane but must be
prepared to make many attempts from many points, and build
things and mend things as we go along. The essential thing is that
we should be going together, in the same direction, and that we get
into step now. Action at the end of the war will fix the pattern of
international relations for many years to come, and in the conditions that will prevail then it is less than likely that we could hold a
peace conference of the habitual kind. Frontiers must be settled,
and there may be some changes; as no change can satisfy both
sides, all one can hope is that frontiers will appear less important
and more acceptable as we organize common action across them.
But for this to be possible, frontiers must be fixed in advance or at
least in the actual armistice, or there will be conflict; and if plans
for common action are not prepared in advance, there will be
chaos—the chaos of many competing and conflicting local actions.
Could a returning Czech or Greek or Polish government tell its
people to be patient and wait till a distant conclave works out
plans for reconstruction?

Co-operation for the common good is the task, both for the sake
of peace and of a better life, and for that it is essential that certain
interests and activities should be taken out of the mood of competition and worked together. But it is not essential to make that co-

operation fast to a territorial authority, and indeed it would be senseless to do so when the number of those activities is limited, while their range is the world. "Economic areas do not always run with political areas," wrote the *New York Times* (February 26, 1943) in commenting on the Alaska Highway scheme, and such cross-country co-operation would simply make frontiers less important. "Apply this principle to certain European areas and the possibilities are dazzling." If it be said that all that may be possible in war but hardly in peace, that can only mean that practically the thing is possible but that we doubt whether in normal times there would be the political will to do it. Now, apart from everything else, the functional method stands out as a solid touchstone in that respect. Promissory covenants and charters may remain a headstone to unfulfilled good intentions, but the functional way is action itself and therefore an inescapable test of where we stand and how far we are willing to go in building up a new international society. It is not a promise to act in a crisis, but itself the action that will avoid the crisis. Every activity organized in that way would be a layer of peaceful life; and a sufficient addition of them would create increasingly deep and wide strata of peace—not the forbidding peace of an alliance, but one that would suffuse the world with a fertile mingling of common endeavor and achievement.

This is not an argument against any ideal of formal union, if that should prove a possible ultimate goal. It is, above all, a plea for the creation now of the elements of an active international society. Amidst the tragedy of war one can glimpse also the promise of a broader outlook, of a much deeper understanding of the issues than in 1918. It is because the peoples are ready for action that they cannot wait. We have no means and no standing to work out some fine constitution and try to impose it in time upon the world. But we do have the standing and the means to prepare for immediate practical action. We do not know what will be the sentiments of the peoples of Europe and of other continents at the end of the war, but we do know what their needs will be. *Any* political scheme would start a disputation; *any* working arrangement would raise a hope and make for confidence and patience.

The functional way may seem a spiritless solution—and so it is, in the sense that it detaches from the spirit the things which are of the body. No advantage has accrued to anyone when economic and other social activities are wedded to fascist or communist or other political ideologies; their progeny has always been confusion and conflict. Let these things appear quite starkly for what they are, practical household tasks, and it will be more difficult to make them into the household idols of "national interest" and "national honor." The ideological movements of our time, because of their indiscriminate zeal, have sometimes been compared to religious movements. They may be, but at their core was not a promise of life hereafter. The things which are truly of the spirit—and therefore personal to the individual and to the nation—will not be less winged for being freed in their turn from that worldly ballast. Hence the argument that opposes democracy to totalitarianism does not call the real issue. It is much too simple. Society is everywhere in travail because it is everywhere in transition. Its problem after a century of laissez faire philosophy is to sift anew, in the light of new economic possibilities and of new social aspirations, what is private from what has to be public; and in the latter sphere what is local and national from what is wider. And for that task of broad social refinement a more discriminating instrument is needed than the old political sieve. In the words of a statement by the American National Policy Committee, "Part of the daring required is the daring to find new forms and to adopt them. We are lost if we dogmatically assume that the procedures of the past constitute the only true expression of democracy."

II
POLITICAL THEORY AND INTERNATIONAL POLITICAL DEVELOPMENT

The Problem
of Equality
in Historical
Perspective

The relative position of states in international politics has been characterized in modern times by a legal principle which has never been practiced and by an actual practice which has never been legalized. Therefore any attempt to set up an organized international system was bound to bring to a head the contradiction between the formal principle of equality of states and the actual predominance of the Great Powers; and both the Covenant of the League and the Charter of the United Nations had to devise a compromise between the legal fiction and the political reality.

General opinion has been apt to denounce such compromise as

This paper was written for the third world congress of the International Political Science Association, Stockholm, August 1955. It attempts to show how the historical evolution of the central democratic tenet, from legal through political to social equality, could now be reproduced also in international society through the use of functional arrangements.

an abuse of an established principle and, of course, of the democratic idea. We as students have on our part not done enough to
clarify the true nature of the problem. We have not done enough to
disentangle the differences and the similarities between closed national communities and the incipient international society; and
more particularly, to assess these divergencies in the light of the
new social outlook which is concerned with equality not of status,
but of opportunity for a good life.

The argument here put forward is that in modern times the
international world has shown a constant advance toward real
equality between states; that, especially within the past few years,
both the pace and the nature of that advance have shown a close
parallel with the social trend which is advancing equality within
national communities; and that any attempt to play up the formal
principle of state equality, like insistence on rigid sovereignty,
would actually block that line of advance.

Equality in the public field has three aspects, each with its own
line of evolution: (1) *legal*—equality before the law; (2) *political*
—equal voice in the making of law; (3) *social*—equality of opportunity in the enjoyment of the benefits of communal life.

Certain general propositions can be advanced in regard to these
several aspects of equality. First, the three aspects also represent
three consecutive stages in political evolution, though the time
intervals between them were unequal and also varied from country
to country. Second, none of them was granted or achieved in one
fell swoop, but rather by gradual steps. We can see this, as regards
legal equality, in the change from aristocratic or clerical privileges
and immunities to the absolute equality of all citizens before the
law of the land; and, on the political side, from restricted aristocratic or other councils, through assemblies based on property or
tax or other limited franchise, to universal suffrage—with a corresponding widening of the functions and powers of the representative bodies. The third, equality of opportunity, is only now being

pressed forward by various means and at various speeds, and is still only in mid-passage even in highly developed Western countries.

What is the position in regard to these three aspects and stages of equality in the international sphere?

History shows that *legal equality* did not exist in the earlier stages of municipal systems and that it was attained slowly and for long only imperfectly as law developed. In the world of states that course was reversed. Because of the great influence of doctrine in the formative period of the modern state system, absolute equality was set up as a fundamental postulate even while international law was still in a rudimentary state. Generally it actually preceded the similar advance in the municipal sphere: States were often equal in international law long before individuals were equal before their country's law.

As a principle, therefore, legal equality is fully established in the international sphere. Any people which succeeds in setting up its own state becomes *ipso facto* the equal of all other sovereign states in international law. For the principle to become an active possession something more is needed, however; it depends inevitably on the coming into being of an effective universal legal system, with authority behind it, which would check the dominance of arbitrary power. The precocious legal perfection has had in fact some disturbing effects on the political side. The history of international relations reflects a continuous struggle to adapt the formal legal principle to a working political reality.[1]

The historical evolution of relations between large and small states forms a fairly definite sequence which shows clearly the line

---

[1] There were two related sides to that process. One was the gradual rise of a positive legal system; the other was the limitations upon state sovereignty involved in the creation of any common authority. The political aspect is, as always, a mixture of legislative and executive functions; and in the international as in the municipal sphere the two are now often linked together in new administrative arrangements.

of advance toward *political equality,* especially in the period between the Peace of Westphalia and the setting up of the United
Nations. One might present that evolution in the shape of a historical tableau, in seven very broad but well-defined scenes:

1. *The common superior.* When Rome stood alone there was
no problem of state relations; Roman civil law turned nations into
citizens of Rome. The idea of unity dominated the Middle Ages,
with its local feudalism—there was no sense as yet of "state" or
"people"—so that with the decay of the Eastern Empire that idea
continued in the partnership of two superiors, pope and emperor.
But that dual expression of the idea declined continuously as a
source of effective authority, and with the collapse of the Holy
Roman Empire there was no hope left of a return to a unitary
system.

2. *Anarchic interlude.* It was in fact followed by an outburst of
political fission. According to Nys, there were in the sixteenth
century some two thousand "sovereign" units in Europe. They
arose and perished, united and divided in wholly arbitrary ways,
but in time a few powerful states emerged gradually out of that
political welter.

3. *State individualism.* Reformation and Renaissance helped to
crystallize out of that shapeless amalgam a new political conception. If world unity under a common superior was not possible, the
only alternative was a society of individual units under some
common law and purpose. Bodin, Puffendorf, and Grotius, above
all, were responsible for working out a doctrinal basis for that
incipient political outlook.

4. *Balance of power.* The new state individualism was confirmed politically at the Peace of Westphalia, when for the first
time all the states met to settle the affairs of Europe together. That
meeting in common in no way implied, however, any sense of and
for an international society, though it did imply an admission that
utter detachment was practically not possible. In the absence of

formal rules and of a formal authority, the new individualism was thrown back upon the pragmatic method of a balance of power. Political units began to combine for the protection of their interests and to balance their influence. The balance of power thus came to provide a rough working system with a fairly clear general purpose.

5. *Directorate of Great Powers.* That pragmatic system was badly shaken by the French Revolution and the Napoleonic wars. They showed the frightened monarchs the need for some organization to watch over and guide the progress of international society.

a. *The Congress of Vienna.* This was a first attempt to bring all European states together in conference with the intention of doing so periodically. But conditions were not yet ripe for some such common authority through common counsel. The Holy Alliance was at best a benevolent despotism of a few Great Powers, the smaller states being ignored. Moreover, instead of guiding international progress, it fell into an attempt to check the new popular current and its revolutionary threat to legitimism. The consequence was a full return to individualism (when laissez faire, it must be remembered, permeated the general outlook of the time).

b. *Concert of Europe.* But two new powerful forces were gathering strength: the idea of nationality, with its explosive possibilities, and at the same time the tremendous economic changes and expansion which broke through state individualism and gave some seers, like Adam Smith and Cobden, a vision of a new organic international unity. In the face of such formidable trends the Great Powers found themselves forced to join hands so as to restrain the one and to guide the other, and thus to act gradually as a *Concert of Europe.* But the Concert was not, and was never meant to be, an organized system. Indeed, the intervention of the Powers was not only infrequent but reluctant, and then only to try to keep the peace among competing national ambitions, with inevitably a strong bias toward maintaining the status quo. The Powers preferred to act at need as an informal committee; they denied any idea that they formed or claimed anything like a collective authority, being themselves unprepared to submit to any common system.

In the meantime the intense growth of economic and social relations since the Congress of Vienna was producing a need to build up binding international rules. Congresses and conferences were called together for the purpose, but common rules were difficult to establish without a common political system. Hence the need for joint action was met through two alternative means: by the conclusion of a mass of treaties and conventions (900 between 1874 and 1883 were gathered in one collection alone), limited in scope and in time, like private contracts between individual states; and by attempts to develop elements of international administration (the International Postal Union was the first) rather than legislation. Some thirty such international bodies were working smoothly and efficiently on the eve of the First World War.

In these ways the nineteenth century came to show a rising sense of the international community of interest, a change in outlook that was the main advance in a hundred years. Together with the increase in the number of states and the growth of democratic sentiment, that sense led at the turn of the century to the idea of some form of orderly international society, to embrace not merely Europe but the states of the world at large.

6. *The common council.* Political equality can be achieved only within an organized political society, but no such attempt was made during the nineteenth century. The growing trend toward joint policy and action was bound to benefit the weaker states indirectly, but they were allowed little share in major political decisions.

The Hague conferences of 1899 and 1907 therefore represented a crucial milestone: from the directorate of the Great Powers to an assembly of all independent states; from oligarchic to democratic decisions; from accident to system, the purpose of the conferences being to create permanent common rules and organs of action. This was the first opportunity the small states had to play an active part, but their eagerness to use the occasion rather as a chance to assert their formal equality produced a deadlock and so left the Hague conferences to mean politically more by what they implied than by what they achieved.

The Versailles Conference was a mixture of the old and the new (though admittedly war settlements are always arbitrary). The small states were present but were not allowed to play any part in the commissions dealing with territorial issues; while the plenary sessions in which they participated merely registered decisions already taken. The Council of Ten—the real decisions having been made by the Big Four—was continued by a limited Council of Ambassadors.

7. *The common polity.* It was left to the first two great experiments in international organization to bring to a head the line of advance toward political equality, but both also revealed the complexity of the issues involved in it. To allow the outline of the historical evolution to appear more clearly, only the relevant aspects of their constitutional arrangements will be indicated at this point.

a. *The League of Nations.* The first attempt to organize an international polity approached the problem of equality with much hesitation. The so-called House-Wilson draft meant to bring only the Great Powers into some kind of association; the Hurst-Miller draft provided for a council of Great Powers which would dominate the League;[2] as regards both structure and powers the final

[2] Colonel E. M. House, personal adviser to President Wilson; Sir Cecil Hurst and David Hunter Miller, legal advisers respectively to the English and American delegations at the Paris Peace Conference.

Covenant was in fact more democratic. The League Assembly was fully democratic; the Council was oligarchic, but all members were eligible and all were entitled to sit when directly concerned. The Court of International Justice was open to all states; in the League's administrative bodies there was full equality of rights.

b. *The United Nations*. One preliminary aspect is worth noting: For the first time such a vital international project was thrown open for public discussion (eight months) before being adopted by governments, and also for the first time private bodies (non-governmental associations) were given a formal right to express an informed opinion on both the constitution and the working arrangements of the United Nations.

The United Nations General Assembly is fully democratic and has greater powers than had the Assembly of the League. The Security Council is still oligarchic and has wider powers; but above all the abandonment of the unanimity rule means a revolutionary advance, the majority being composed of smaller states, even if this is balanced by the veto allowed to the five Great Powers in certain limited and specified issues. The Economic and Social Council is fully democratic, no special position being provided for the Great Powers. The International Court is fully democratic. The special agencies and other administrative bodies are fully democratic. Moreover, all these administrative units are provided with functional assemblies of their own, in which groups and interests directly concerned are represented on an equal footing—an arrangement which so far is in advance of even national developments (e.g., no representative element has been provided in Britain or elsewhere for autonomous nationalized services, nor in the U.S. for the TVA).

c. *The European Coal and Steel Community*. Finally, the first great experiment in supra-national administration represents an alternative mode of achieving political equality. Though the Authority controls vital sectors in the economic life of the six member countries, its organs are based on full equality (with a few secondary reservations) between its members. Indeed, the judicial function goes even further, as the judges of the court need not be nationals of the member states—a first glimmer, this, of international citizenship, of international responsibility. Such a free and positive political equality no doubt was possible because, as in the special agencies, the field of activity and therefore the powers of the authority are strictly defined and limited.

To political scientists it is a commonplace that formal rules often mean less than the way the system works; actual political practice depends on the general outlook and on the social maturity of a particular society. Many new states have perfect constitutions, while political practice lags far behind. But in the international sphere it is on the whole true that actual practice has rather improved on the formal advance noted before. The historical picture has shown a clear evolution from the absolutism of the common superior to the present experiment with an organic representative system. The change in outlook was part of the liberal-democratic trend of the nineteenth century. Nations, like individuals, acquired rights of citizenship without regard to wealth or strength, and in both spheres there was a gradual increase in the number of enfranchised citizens.

At the same time industrial revolution and economic expansion, which were creating a new class of wealth, also added great strength to a few Great Powers, and that did not incline them to favor international control; it was in fact the period during which they competed for colonial expansion, as in the scramble for Africa. But the small states were no less shy of extraneous authority and jealous of their new independence and formal equality (as the new Asian, Middle Eastern, and African states are at the present time). Hence the first view taken of liberty was negative, alike in the national and in the international spheres. Only gradually was it

replaced in both, and in politics as in economics, by a more positive view—one which looked to a common interest and to a common responsibility exercised through a common authority. Such a
change from a negative to a positive view of government was
necessary before the smaller states could find scope to share in
political influence. In that respect the working of the League and
of the United Nations quickly showed, and in a number of ways,
the great change in their position.

In both organizations the administrative personnel have increasingly acquired the character of a civil service, with a corresponding
regard for individual rather than national qualifications. Though
the administrative head of the United Nations is more influential
than he was in the League, so far the secretaries-general have been
chosen from small nations. Working arrangements have given
small states a considerable share in official positions; a larger
number of chairmen for the various committees are chosen from
the smaller states than from among the Great Powers. One other
development which has added to this progressive trend is the new
type of international conferences. Most of these are now technical
conferences at which expert competence counts above all; while
their subject matter and conclusions are directed toward common
needs and benefits, rather than aiming, as of old, at an increase in
political power through diplomatic bargaining, from which the
major states inevitably profited most.

The smaller states themselves have contributed to this change in
the balance of power in yet another way. They have often acted in
regional groups—such as the Little Entente, Latin America, and
now the Arab, Southeast Asian, and African groups—which have
given them correspondingly greater strength in discussion and voting. Above all, in the new international forum they have as often
acquired great influence through the character and personality of
their representatives—such men as Nansen, Branting, Hymans,
Hambro, Loudon, Beneš—and not merely in matters of special

interest to them but, more significantly, even in general international issues. The full publicity attending such debates has indeed on more than one important occasion made these men into spokesmen of world opinion, which they were sometimes able to lead against the narrower policy of the Great Powers.

The essence of democratic equality, political machinery apart, is that laws and rules should be the same for all. The growth of such common rules—whether as international law, as multilateral treaties, through joint controls and administration—in place of one-sided diplomatic bargainings implies a degree of consent for their adoption. It also implies submission to a common judgment for interpretation and execution and to that extent, therefore, a shift from the rule of power to the rule of law in international affairs. We have, indeed, advanced so far within one generation that we now take it for granted that international action in any particular issue or field must apply to large and small states alike. Even if there is not yet full equality in the actual making of policy, a policy that would confer privileges on the great and powerful is now hardly conceivable; and for the rest, there is actual political equality for executive and judicial purposes.

Apart from general international law, small beginnings with the provision of common rules were made in the last century: e.g., in 1805 at the Congress of Vienna in relation to inland waterways; at Paris in 1856 and at Berlin in 1878, in regard to the treatment of religious minorities; at Brussels in 1884, with regard to expansion in Africa. Rules for conduct in war, for arbitration, etc., were agreed upon at the Hague in 1899 and 1907, with many other additions since then. But the making of general and permanent rules could become an accepted normal procedure only with the setting up of a regular authority. From the history of the League of Nations two examples might be cited as characteristic: the minorities and the mandates systems. Critics have rightly objected that the minorities system (which penetrated into the domestic sphere of the states affected) was imposed only upon some small states. But on the other hand, the mandates system applied only to large states and, indeed, to states which had just won a great war and so were imposing that restraint upon themselves. Moreover, while both the minorities and the mandates system came under international control, that control was more stringent in regard to mandates; and while the minorities system in effect only served to protect a status quo, the mandates system was meant ultimately to extinguish the rule of the imperial Powers in the mandate territories altogether.

That was a very impressive example of peaceful change. A crucial new principle was indeed proclaimed in Article XIX of the League of Nations Covenant. This referred to the peaceful revision of treaties and damaging conditions—the principle that conflict could be avoided not by continuously changing frontiers (or political allegiance) but by adapting and improving relations within and across those frontiers. The social theory implicit in Article XIX thus brought international outlook very close to the philosophy which underlies the purpose of national society.

The rising trend toward establishing in international relations the rule of law and subduing the rule of power was the necessary foundation for a true legal and political equality of states. It is also in keeping with the historical evolution within individual nations. But the line of advance favored in our own time is through social equality. Political equality is no longer looked upon as an end in itself but as a means toward a better society, to be used not merely for preserving general abstract rights but for acquiring specific concrete rights, according to needs and aspirations. When applied to the international sphere, the trend reveals an astonishing change within the past generation or so, a change which has produced a sense of mutual social responsibility in a world that politically is still divided in a mass of independent units. A small beginning was made about a century ago, in a sporadic way, with the setting up of various international unions whose services, whatever the difference in financial contributions, were available to all members on equal terms. That beneficent practice thus equalized the position of member countries in the field covered by the service; and this was all the more valuable because some of the smaller states might not have been able to have the service at all without such international organization. Under the League of Nations that line of action grew considerably—with such things as economic information and services, League loans, the Bank of International Settlements, the International Mortgage Bank, health service, relief work, the ILO, and other practical activities, and in some of these even the U.S. was willing to participate. That was one of the reasons why the Bruce Report, in 1939, urged the expansion of this line of work as the most promising way of giving scope and strength to the League.[3]

It is indeed in that direction that international society has progressed more rapidly and effectively since the establishment of the United Nations, with its Economic and Social Council. These communal activities are now so much taken for granted that we hear relatively little about them, in contrast with the endless and vociferous debates which becloud most political issues. The valuable work carried out by various agencies under the general name of technical assistance now covers the world and almost every sector of economic and social development. These agencies bring to small or underdeveloped countries means and experience which otherwise they could not command for a long time to come. Moreover, by training experts from among their own nationals it also enables those countries in their turn gradually to take part on an equal

---

[3] *The Development of International Co-operation in Economic and Social Affairs,* Bruce Report (Geneva, 1939); League of Nations Document 1939, General 3. "The primary object of international co-operation should be rather mutual help than reciprocal contract—above all, the exchange of knowledge and of the fruits of experience" (p. 11).

footing of individual ability, not of national power, in the administration of international services and agencies.

Where the agency is truly supra-national, as in the case of the European Coal and Steel Community, the process of social equalization has full scope (including such a remarkable breaking into the domestic sphere as the transfer of displaced workers to new positions abroad). No doubt these activities could be improved and extended. But the point is that in their outlook and in the way they work they illuminate better than any other change the gulf that separates us from nineteenth-century practice: We are moving from an acquisitive toward a co-operative international society. The world has developed a conscience, and a sense that it is both necessary and right to equalize social conditions between its various parts and peoples—both as a way to peace and as the foundation for a unified common society.

The true nature of the problem of relations between large and small states can be seen only if we measure it not against abstract ideas but against actual historical evolution. The line of evolution, especially from the Congress of Vienna to the League of Nations and the United Nations, reveals a continuous progress toward equality—legally, politically, and socially.

It is no less evident that this process has moved in step with the rise of a sense for international organization. In their modern form the Great Powers came into being after the Napoleonic wars and reached their great economic and military predominance during the nineteenth century; and it may seem curious that the smaller states should have claimed, and in a measure secured, a voice in international life during the same period. Yet that was natural enough. That was the great liberal-democratic era which brought about also within the national state popular enfranchisement and respect for the rights of individual citizens—expressed in the international sphere by the doctrine of non-interference; and the same trend begot a genuine international sense, a sense and a demand for common international organization.

Now we are again in a period of vital transition, when clarity of view is as essential as urgency of will. It would be easy to demonstrate that neither the constitution nor the working of the new international system rest as yet on full democratic equality, but such a formalistic view of the problem is for its purpose misguided. Equality has never been the means to political community, but rather the effect, generally gradual, of political community. The growth of international equality will likewise depend on the growth of an international community; and the end we have to keep before us is not the enthronement of a static formal principle, but the infusion of an active principle of maturity into the relations of states.

If one looks at it in this way, as a matter not of form but of process, it becomes clear that the very progress we have made has changed the nature of the problem and that the habitual contrast between large and small states is now out of date, a residue of the era of power politics. In the process of building up a political community the line of division is no longer between strong and weak, whether individuals or states, but between helpful and obstructive, between responsible and irresponsible elements.

As the present historical task is the creation of an international community, there are above all two aspects of the problem of equality to which political scientists have to address themselves. One is a political-sociological aspect—that is, the given conditions of the problem. At present the main responsibility for building up and maintaining the new international system inevitably lies with the few great states which command great strength and wealth. Any arrangement which brings that great predominance of power under some common restraint, under the rule of a common law, is bound to be a step toward real political equality; and if their great wealth can at the same time be harnessed to the advancement of a common welfare, that will build up also a growing measure of social equality. But neither advance will get very far if the smaller states, many of which are young and inexperienced, were to strain at the formal principle of sovereign equality—which has never been more than an ornament—and insist at this stage that they should enjoy also full equality in decision and control. We as students have therefore a part to play in clarifying the true nature of the issue: that the real and urgent problem for the world is to build up the living elements of an international community rather than to secure formal perfection in its initial constitution.

In relation to this central problem the matter of size and power is not conclusive, either historically or sociologically. If there is no particular virtue in bigness, neither is there any special virtue in smallness. Sociologists have differed on this point as much as lawyers differ on legal points. Gumplowicz, Tarde, Ratzel, Giddings, and others have argued that history has witnessed a constant growth in the size of political aggregates and that this has been a benefit to civilization; Comte, LePlay, Vaccaro, and others have argued rather for the social usefulness of small states. In such a rigid form neither view could be fully substantiated. Professor William Rappard—himself a citizen of the small state of Switzerland —has said that if on the whole small states have been less acquisitive and aggressive, this "is less due to their superior virtue than to their inferior power, . . . not because they are more saintly, but because they are less apt to be successful sinners";[4] and Balkan and Latin American history does not prove even the premise that smaller states have been less acquisitive and aggressive. Now we may be faced with a new test: nuclear weapons will become ever cheaper and easier to manufacture, and a very few of them could do immense destruction. Hence the index of power politics will

---

[4] *Pacifism Is Not Enough,* in *Problems of Peace,* Ninth Series (London, Allen and Unwin, for Geneva Institute of International Relations, 1935), Chapter 2, "Small States in the League of Nations," p. 51.

come to lie not so much in the possession of destructive power as in a readiness to use it.

The second aspect of the problem of equality is political-constitutional, involving the arrangements for representation and decision in international government. These arrangements have to be such as to give the few large states the assurance that they will not be swamped by the many small ones and at the same time give the latter every opportunity to share in the common government. If arrangements for decision and control should not rest on a basis of sheer size and power, neither can they rest on formal equality. The proper basis can only be a capacity to assume responsibility for the work to be done and to administer it for the good of the community. It will not be easy to translate such unstatistical criteria into practical political devices—whether they be regional or functional devolution or something else—but just because it will be difficult this is eminently an issue to be appraised by detached political scientists.

For the original constitution of an international system we cannot in any case use the analogy of unitary (democratic) states— one man, one vote; or at best we would have to refer to the practice of more complex polities, such as federations. If the formal equality of the parts is usually recognized in federations in one chamber, as in the United States Senate, their actual inequality finds expression in another chamber, as in the United States House of Representatives. In the United States the change in the method of electing the President, with his enormous powers, has also meant that the parts are given a voice in decision in relation to their actual inequality (population) rather than to their formal sovereign equality. Admittedly in the international sphere the issue is more awkward because of a long tradition of formal equality among independent states. It is made more complex also by the difficulty of using a uniform system of representation. Apart from differences in the size and population of the parts, we also have to face still older differences in national and historical outlook; and for practical purposes of policy and administration—and for some time to come—also wide differences in political and social experience.

The transition from national to international control of political power and of material resources, on a general basis of equality—not equality of possession, but of opportunity in use—is the most stubborn problem that political society has had to face in its long and restless history. We are not helped in the search for a solution by the old and wide gap between political theory and political fact. That gap must ultimately be bridged if we are to succeed in building up a common political society. But as the end is so high and so difficult, it is not an unprincipled or an unwise compromise in these hesitant early stages to err, if need be, on the side of working democracy rather than of voting democracy. Political scientists have a part to play in this, to help to replace adherence to a rigid and worn-out principle, which was meant to keep the states peacefully apart, with serviceable ideas which will help to bring them actively together. Alone in that way is it possible, without damaging the cultural personality of the individual nations, to organize a common authority and common functions under joint control, and through them work up to a positive operation of international equality.

An Advance
in Democratic
Representation

The increasing use of specialized agencies and other international administrative bodies for various practical matters of common interest raised the question of how public opinion was to find expression in their policy. The United Nations Charter has given a number of private professional associations (the Union of International Associations in Brussels has more than 1,200 members) a formal consultative status with the relevant agencies, and to some others an informal right to be heard. Apart from their immediate purpose these arrangements form an experiment in democratic representation of general theoretical interest when almost everywhere parliamentary representation by the counting of heads is now found wanting.[1]

[1] This article appeared in March 1954 in *International Associations,* the monthly journal of the Union. It was also published in revised form under the title "The International NGO's: Experiment in Representation" in the *Manchester Guardian,* April 10, 1954; under the title "A New Democratic Experiment" in *Review of International Co-operation* (the journal of the International Co-operative Alliance, London), May 1954, in English, French, and German versions; under the original title in *World Mental Health* (the Bulletin of the World Federation for Mental Health, London), August 1954; in French in *International Associations,* October 1954.

The vague clamor we hear all about us for this or that kind of world government has obscured the solid progress made so far toward international government; and the fact that, in one direction at any rate, the present international system is actually in advance of national political organization. Though still merely an embryo, yet it has introduced a valuable experiment in democratic representation—a problem which is worrying students of politics even in the oldest of Western democracies.

Throughout the long period of the liberal struggle for political democracy, popular government was linked inseparably with popular representation. Upon the formal principle of the right to vote was built the confident expectation that once granted it would lead to real democratic government; and so with universal suffrage the victory seemed complete and government of the people by the people achieved. To our dismay we now discover that the liberal representative system is everywhere in difficulties and the principle itself often debased. We see how with every increase in the number of voters and in the size of the constituency the links between people and government become ever thinner and weaker. There is not one country where this problem of democratic government, in its institutional sense, is not causing anxiety, to judge from the endless flow of studies and proposals for remedying that situation; and this without mentioning those countries where democratic arrangements, old or new, have been battered down altogether. I am concerned here only with those countries where the democratic system is accepted and yet where its effectiveness is clearly in question. There is growing evidence of some deficiency in its working all along the chain of the traditional representative system. The mass of the voters find themselves with a lessening influence on parliament, and parliament in its turn with less influence on government. We are not so sure now that mass representation necessarily means effective democracy; and in such circumstances dictatorial regimes from both right and left have been able with some plausibility to usurp the democratic claim by pointing to the mass support they can get for their views and activities.

How has this situation arisen, and what can we do about it? Representation in all democratic states still rests on the basic liberal principle that every qualified citizen should have a voice in the making of the laws and rules by which the life of his country is governed. That was not merely a formal idea to protect him against arbitrary government; it was meant to give the mass of citizens, through their representatives, active initiative in the making of policy and control over its execution. In both respects these traditional assumptions have become so enfeebled as almost to threaten the central principle itself. We have come a long way indeed from the historical town meeting, when all the citizens were assembled together and knew what the issue under discussion was about, and could afterward see with their own eyes how their decisions were carried out. Government activities are now so extensive and so complex that even in parliament only a few members find time to pay attention to any particular proposal, and even fewer can understand it. And while the volume of legislation is increasing in a terrifying way, it has of necessity to be applied uniformly over a wide area and so to be centralized in administration; and more and more of it, for the same reason, is taking the form of "delegated legislation," with details left to be filled in by officials. In many ways we are moving back toward that "administrative state" which was the instrument of benevolent autocracy.

In spite of the general anxiety felt over this decline in the meaning and practice of democratic representation it has hardly been noticed how, in this respect, international development shows an advance over national politics. When those who drafted the Charter of the United Nations brought, in its Article 71,[2] private inter-

---

[2] Article 71 reads: "The Economic and Social Council may make suitable arrangements for consultation with non-governmental organizations which are concerned with matters within its competence. Such arrange-

national organizations into a formal relationship with the constitutional organs of the United Nations, they were assumed merely to
have taken over and given a regular form to what had been a
hesitant practice in the working of the League of Nations. In fact
they did very much more. Whether knowingly or not, they took an
important step toward a possible modern solution of the problem
of democratic representation.

As the British Parliament is the mother of parliaments, and
Britain has a justified reputation for political good sense, because
of a readiness to adapt political institutions pragmatically to
changing needs and conditions, the contrast between the United
Nations and British practice is especially striking. The social experiment known in Britain as "nationalizaton" was intended to put
some important sectors of economic life under public ownership
and control. As regards ownership that purpose has been achieved,
but as regards control the unexpected and paradoxical effect has
been rather to deprive Parliament of its constitutional function and
powers over these very sectors of economic life. As with the
famous TVA, each of the British nationalized industries and services is under the management of an autonomous board or authority; and while that functional autonomy is rightly regarded as
essential for efficient management, as it neutralizes political interference, it has virtually created sectors of national life from which
democratic initiative and control are excluded. No one intended
such a result. That is precisely why it provides striking evidence
that the traditional democratic arrangements are not always com-
patible with the range and problems of government in the new
social state.

The problem, therefore, is how to re-establish as far as possible
democratic initiative and control in policy, whatever the political

---

ments may be made with international organizations and, where appropriate, with national organizations after consultation with the member of
the United Nations concerned."

device employed. One obvious way would seem to be to associate every public activity with a body of opinion from experts who really know what the scope of legislation in that particular field should be, and who also have the knowledge and the direct interest to watch, on behalf of the political community at large, how policy is carried out in that field. Is not this precisely what the new arrangements under the United Nations provide in the international sphere? For the discussion of general ideas there are the Assembly and the Economic and Social Council. But the significant innovation is that every one of the specialized agencies, including the ILO, has what one might call its own little functional parliament, which meets periodically and lays down policy, establishes the budget, and on the next occasion reviews the execution of that policy. In a more definite way the idea of such a functional parliament was incorporated in the European Coal and Steel Community.

It is especially in connection with the defined activities of these specialized agencies that non-governmental organizations have an extremely valuable part to play. Through them democratic initiative and democratic control could be re-established and canalized in an effective way. After the First World War, under the pressure of the new tasks of government, there was a good deal of interest in the idea of economic parliaments, and they were in fact tried in Germany and elsewhere. The experiment proved a failure. In the first place, it is not possible nowadays to separate economics from politics and general social issues; then, too, these economic parliaments were as mixed and inchoate in their knowledge and experience and interests as are the traditional political assemblies. The field over which they were supposed to exercise authority was much too wide, and the advice they were supposed to offer was much too mixed to be closely relevant to the highly specialized duties of government departments and other public bodies. Above all, in economic parliaments the several groups were there to fight for sectional interests, much as in any ordinary parliament, whereas functional bodies represent one interest and one purpose common to them all, and the debate is about ways and means.

In the light of such experience, and in view of the tremendous increase in the business of government since the Second World War, the idea of a European parliament, let alone of a world parliament, elected by universal suffrage and acting on behalf of and for enormous constituencies, is dangerously unrealistic. A continental or a world assembly might perhaps find a momentary unity of view under the impetus of some strong emotional issue; it could never express practically and continuously the views of hundreds of millions on the ever-changing business of life and government when even national parliaments have difficulty in reflecting a true public opinion and exercising a true democratic control.

The existence of widespread non-governmental organizations provides a sound alternative for the development of an informed international opinion in particular fields. Such organizations could be made into instruments of really informed democratic representation, whereas the mass collection of millions of votes by universal suffrage would in truth represent no clear opinion on anything. At present the United Nations and the specialized agencies represent mainly inter-governmental arrangements; therefore it is perhaps inevitable that official delegates should have the main voice in shaping their policy—though this is not exclusively so, and the ILO, at least, makes constitutional provision for the representation of organized labor. In every country, paradoxical though this may seem, the more the activities of the state increase, the greater becomes the need for informed private groups to have a part in shaping policy and exercising control over those activities. In the same way, the more we develop joint international activities, the greater will obviously be the need and scope for the relevant non-governmental organizations to be associated with those activities.

On their side, if the non-governmental organizations are to become the accepted channel of international public opinion, they will have to display a sense of restraint and responsibility in their views and claims, and perhaps also perform among themselves a certain process of selection. There are too many which still seem to think that the bravest achievement in every instance is to put forward the most extreme possible case, supported by the loudest possible clamor. Apart from that, international authority cannot and will not listen seriously to a whole congeries of groups with all their mixed views on a particular issue. If there are too many voices shouting at the same time to different purpose, then nothing very clear will be audible in the clamor.

From that point of view it is possible to question whether the element of rigidity in the present selection of non-governmental organizations and their division into fixed categories is really the best way of dealing with the very fluid growth of non-political international activities. But that is probably not so much a matter of making constitutional changes as of promoting a sensible and elastic practice—a practice which might develop into a custom of calling in, when and as it may seem desirable, those private groups whose knowledge and experience and representative character seem most appropriate to the specific issue.

There is one other aspect of this possible development which is of importance. In the excitement of becoming potent instruments in the making of formal policy, the non-governmental organizations, if they are to survive, must never forget that they must act, so to speak, as a two-way channel: It is as important for them to bring back to the general public information on what their particular specialized agency is doing, and make clear the reasons for it, as to act as the voice of that public opinion at the seat of power. If they fail in this, and become merely specialized pressure groups, they will before long become as much strangers to the general public as government officials now tend to be. Then it will be left to some other instrument at some other level to come into being and perform the function of public education which they will have lost by default. Their strength can at all times be only the strength of the informed opinion which they themselves create. But if they do their part well, each non-governmental organization, in the words of Dr. Lyman White, would "contribute a segment of world unity for the particular interest with which it deals."[3] And, one might add, an accumulation of such segments of international unity is the only way to create a living and lasting world community.

[3] *International Non-governmental Organizations: Their Purposes, Methods and Accomplishments* (New Brunswick, Rutgers University Press, 1951), p. 12.

Problems in International Administration

Advances in policy and government within a state generally come about through the interplay of popular demand and political leadership. That has rarely been the way with progress in international government; whatever measure of common action has been achieved since the rise of the modern national movements has been rather against the grain of general sentiment and policy. Every step toward international co-operation has been contested, sometimes retracted, and made firm eventually only under pressure of necessity. We have seen this happen in our own time. Yet never has the need for joint international action, as distinct from political alliances, been more evident than during the two world wars and the great economic depression between them, and never has joint action gone further than during these two wars. But the circum-

This paper was prepared for a conference on international administration organized jointly by the Institute of Public Administration and the Royal Institute of International Affairs in 1945. It first appeared in *Public Administration* (London), 1945, and was reprinted in booklet form with other conference papers under the title *International Administration*, published by the IPA in 1945.

stances that occasioned that action also showed up the halting attitude of governments and public opinion. In 1918 the effective inter-Allied war controls were hastily broken up on the morrow of the Armistice, with total disregard for the needs of reconstruction. When former President Hoover said that the idea of continued joint action filled him with "complete horror," he was merely putting a personal accent upon a general attitude. During the great depression of the 1930's national leaders everywhere insisted that the trouble was due to extraneous causes beyond their control. But instead of following the logic of that remarkable admission that even great and rich countries could no longer control their own fate, they turned inward into the fold of national planning.

A change in that general attitude is more opportune now than it might have been in 1919 or 1930; it is also more urgent. We shall be faced everywhere, and in Europe especially, with desperately heavy tasks of reconstruction which can be done satisfactorily only through joint action. Second, and more encouragingly, there is now the determined interest of the masses everywhere in social improvement and security. There is one other and very considerable point: The new sense of responsibility in the West toward undeveloped areas provides an exceptional need and scope for international action. Unless help to those areas is made a matter of joint concern, the "rich man's burden" will only breed rivalry between the Powers in the Middle East, in Asia, and in Latin America. In all these directions it is patent that joint international action would be more effective than separate national action, and that international plans must be set in motion before national plans and national action have had a chance to harden.

As these new needs and opportunities require closer international co-operation than in the past, they will also require new and suitable types of international administration. Broadly and briefly, we have to move on from piecemeal and sporadic international co-operation to forms of continuous international government. The change in outlook that is needed might be illustrated by the case of the rehabilitation loans of the League of Nations. In principle they were a vast improvement on the haphazard loans, often with political strings, formerly made from government to government. The League loans to Austria, to Hungary, etc., were granted after inquiries by a body of international experts. The money was raised internationally, and its use was supervised by agents of the League. Yet all that international machinery was put to work only to strengthen separate national economies; there was no attempt at helping each by furthering co-operation among them all. This is not a criticism of those who had a part in this altruistic work, let alone a criticism of the League of Nations. The point is that at the time our outlook was obviously not mature enough; we could still see international action only in terms of national use. Now we begin to realize that an international system which is to last and grow must take over and co-ordinate certain activities hitherto in the keeping of the national state; just as the state, for its new ends, has increasingly to take over activities from local bodies. The range of these activities would indeed be new, and forms of government will have to fit the varied political fabric of the world of states.

In the past, when states were largely self-contained, the ordinary diplomatic and consular machinery was enough for handling the limited transactions between them. But during the nineteenth century the opening of new lands, the discovery of new materials, the tremendous development in communications made the peoples of the world truly inter-dependent. While these developments unified the world materially they also divided it politically into a growing number of independent sovereign states, and the working of these two opposite trends complicated as much as it enriched the content of international relations. That is easily seen from the variety of problems, new or newly recognized, to which the machinery of international relations had to be adapted.

The new needs were met at first by the growing practice of holding international conferences, but two points might be noted about them. First, the great official conferences were almost wholly concerned with politico-diplomatic affairs. There were no attempts in the economic field to build up something like a European watch committee, like the Concert of Europe; nor, like the effort of the Hague conferences, to work out a system of international law and order. Even after the First World War the international problem was regarded as essentially a matter of making the world safe for free national enterprise and competition, for international laissez faire. Second, and reflecting the same attitude, even essential common needs were obstructed for the sake of private national interests or prestige. Britain opposed joint action for dealing with epidemics out of fear that her shipping might be hampered; Germany and Austria refused to join the International Public Health Office because it was set up in Paris; and so on—attitudes which must now appear to us hardly less peculiar than the jealous concern of seventeenth- and eighteenth-century ambassadors with precedence for their coaches in the streets of Western capitals.

The practice of meeting in conference was evidence of a growing sense that the international affairs with which they dealt could not be left to chance. Indirectly this was shown also, as the century wore on, in the changing character of these conferences. They ceased to be gatherings of kings and princes and instead brought together the responsible ministers who represented a country's policy rather than a ruler's will, and who were bent upon reaching agreements which would work. These early attempts at international co-operation did not always achieve results, largely because there was no machinery for carrying out their decisions. The next stage was marked by efforts to secure, by various means, continuity in policy and follow-up in action. Instead of being called *ad hoc* conferences tended to become periodical, like the Hague conferences; they also became more technical in their approach. Often a small staff was engaged in preparing the work of the conference and afterward in putting its decisions into effect; and in a number of cases small permanent bodies were set up which functioned in the periods between the general conferences.

One of the characteristics of international action in the last century, indeed, was the growth of unions or bureaus, usually set up by an international conference convened for that purpose and entrusted with specific responsibilities and with permanent machinery for carrying out its work and for securing necessary changes. The International Telegraph Union (1865) was among the first, but perhaps the best known and the most successful is the Universal Postal Union (1875). The need here was obvious and the work of benefit to all—yet even so there was at first opposition lest the existence of the Union should encroach upon the sovereignty of member states. Two points are especially worth noting about this service: The first is that it continued even during the two world wars. Postal services between enemy countries were carried on through neutral lines and everywhere were resumed automatically as soon as the fighting ceased. Second, the service has in a way become a fragment of international government. It links up, in a chain of their own, the foreign mail divisions of the national post offices, which to that degree and for that purpose form something like a world service with an administration and function of its own. One could mention, of course, a good many other unions, institutes, and bureaus with differing constitutions and tasks, some of which have not prospered like the Postal Union; but they are sufficiently well known, and here we are interested more in the general trend of international administration.

During the nineteenth century a great number of private international bodies also came into being in varying forms and with a variety of objectives. These private bodies generally used the conference method, with a general assembly in which all members were represented, a small executive to act between sessions, often with a permanent bureau to maintain continuity. The rapid developments of the past 150 years have indeed transformed the whole substance of international relations, not only by creating new problems but also by quickening, on a social plane, the sense of international community. Many of the facilities in communications, etc., upon which a modern country depends have been secured through international action, and the barriers of technical complexities which in such matters might have obstructed agreement have been broken down through the co-operation of experts with a lively sense both of the difficulty and of the necessity of agreement. The growth of such regular practical collaboration, like the earlier change from royal to ministerial conferences, led to a corresponding change in the personnel engaged in this work. "The trend of international administration during the past twenty-five years," wrote Gordon Shipman, "has been away from political and diplomatic influence. More and more organizations are being set up on the theory that purely technical problems can be separated from political problems, and that technical co-operation on the part of national administrative services can be brought about successfully in the international sphere without the interference of the political departments of the member states."[1] This has led to the increased use of technical instead of diplomatic personnel as members of international conferences and institutions; more significantly, it has brought about within the countries concerned a growing devolution in the conduct of their international affairs.

This tendency toward decentralization in foreign relations is apparent in two directions: First, negotiations on many questions which involve foreign agreements have tended to break away from diplomatic offices and methods; second, changes in national prac-

[1] "International Administrative Unions" (privately communicated paper, 1932). See, for the general trend, "1957 International Associations since the Congress of Vienna" (Association of International Unions, Brussels, 1957).

tice arising out of such agreements often had to be reported to the international agency concerned and thus, in a sense, came under its supervision. The change was discussed with reference to Great Britain in a valuable article by the late Dr. S. H. Bailey of the University of London. He noted that the growth of international intercourse "is raising new problems and, in soliciting solutions which must from the nature of the problems be international, has encouraged this process of throwing upon the several government departments certain tasks which bring them into official contact with foreign governments and international organizations."[2] Postal, maritime, sanitary, and other services in the various countries can thus discuss and settle their technical problems directly, without passing through the complicating network of diplomatic and political censors. The practice of direct communication and collaboration between the permanent officials and experts of the several national administrations is necessary for good performance; it also helps to develop a healthy international sense among those national civil services. In this way the ground is being prepared for the seemingly inevitable development of an international section within each of the national departments.

Foreign offices often are now left merely with the function of registering agreements concluded by separate departments; even when diplomatic channels are still used, technical details are prepared by the competent departments. "Gaps in the wisdom of the Foreign Office are more clearly realized as international relations grow more technically complex."[3] The practice has been hampered by the traditional conservatism of foreign offices, unwilling to surrender their role of having a say in all that happens beyond the border; and especially when some dispute arises, the tendency is to pull it back into diplomatic channels. But, as Dr. Bailey said,

[2] "Devolution in the Conduct of International Relations," *Economica* (London), November 1930, p. 268.
[3] *Ibid.*, p. 265.

"the conception of 'foreign policy' as a clearly enunciated set of principles consistently applied by the Foreign Secretary and his subordinates during the lifetime of the government has become largely a fiction. The modern state is brought into contact with other states in almost every aspect of its national existence; . . . the strands of modern international relations spread to every nook and cranny of the governmental machine and weave a pattern as complex as that of domestic administration."[4]

This tendency was quickened by the needs of the First World War, when urgency of action mattered more than protocol and thus led to direct contact between responsible officials. Almost all the conferences on post-war problems were manned by competent experts from appropriate departments, and the relegation of such problems to the calmer atmosphere of technical discussion was greatly encouraged also through the work of the League of Nations. It is significant that at recent conferences called together to prepare plans for post-war international co-operation in the economic and social fields (Hot Springs, Atlantic City, Bretton Woods, etc.) the British Foreign Office was either not represented at all or, by courtesy, only through observers.

The League of Nations, whatever else it may have done, was not effective in the field of economic co-operation, and the spectacular attempt of the World Monetary and Economic Conference (London, 1933) to work out an international economic policy also broke down completely. That suggests that the old expedients are no longer enough for present needs and conditions. The reasons are not far to seek. Economic problems have become more intense and complex because their solution must now satisfy also an intense social purpose. Hence economic action is now planned, and in one way or another controlled, by the state and so becomes in fact a political process. Many activities which in the nineteenth century were carried on freely by private groups and bodies are

[4] *Ibid.,* p. 273.

now taken over or controlled by national authorities. Unless, therefore, the new arrangements are co-ordinated internationally, political control must cause some of those activities to lapse or to shrink, so that in this respect we would be moving backward. Problems raised by the free economy of the nineteenth century could be dealt with by sporadic co-operation, but those created by the controlled national economies of the twentieth century can be met only by equally planned international co-operation. There has to be a working affinity between the general nature of national economies and that of international economic arrangements.[5]

To meet the needs and the effects of modern economic and technical developments and the new ideas of social responsibility, industrial countries are having recourse increasingly to delegated legislation and administrative law. Such legislation deals not with essential principles of a democratic society which were at issue during the past century but with practical aspects, apt to change frequently and rapidly; hence the daily task of application has to be delegated to administrative bodies which make the detailed rules and modify them as new situations require. All these circumstances are reproduced in the international field, and so, in a growing measure, have to be the devices for dealing with them. International administrative agencies have often had to be given power to make and amend rules, a power which sometimes has simply grown out of their activities. But development has been rather haphazard, and this has irked many people into demanding an authority which would bring some order into the working of this motley of international agencies and activities. There is a risk, however, that in pursuing perfection of form we may put a constraint upon the working realities of the slowly emerging international community. It is already evident, for instance, that nations are more ready to grant executive authority to international bodies

[5] See David Mitrany, "The International Consequences of National Planning," *Yale Review,* September 1947.

if the latter have particular and strictly defined functions. Mr. M. R. K. Burge has drawn attention to the fact that even within the limited framework of the ILO a similar specialization of functions has been found more effective: "In general, therefore, it seems possible to say that the tendency now is to diminish the insistence upon exact uniformity of conditions as the goal, to attach less importance therefore to the legal processes of ratification, and to devolve some of the functions of the Conference to specialized bodies of a more or less similar composition."[6]

The need for international agencies with executive power itself postulates that their functions must be clearly defined and limited. On the other hand, the varied nature of the problems to be dealt with seems to require an equal flexibility in administrative structure and methods. The worst thing we could do would be to try to force these international arrangements into some general mold, to give priority to form over performance, or to press for action before the need for it is generally accepted. The need for the joint control of epidemics has been clearly proved; the need for some joint control of civil aviation is widely anticipated; the need for joint economic development, especially of more backward areas, may be obvious but has not yet taken shape. Flexibility in administration is therefore essential from the nature of these matters. It is also important because in many cases international action may still have to be carried out through national agencies, and there is an infinite variation between, for instance, Soviet controls and relatively free economies, between unitary states like France and federal states like America.

As concrete examples we might consider three types of international authority, the nature of each being related to the nature of its function: advisory and co-ordinating international authorities,

[6] "Some Aspects of Administration in the International Labour Office," in *International Administration* (London, Institute of Public Administration, 1945), p. 25.

where both the performance and the means for it remain mainly under national control (the organization contemplated at the Hot Springs Conference for agriculture would seem to be of this type); an international authority with control over distribution, where some general material (essential minerals, rubber, oil, etc.), limited in supply or in its geographical distribution, is needed by all countries for national use; an international agency with direct administrative control over an activity or a service which itself would be international—such as long-range aviation, oceanic or Danubian shipping, or regional land transport, etc., in Europe or South America. Security might also be considered as a function falling within the last category.

It will be a matter of international statesmanship to safeguard such experiments from overstrain, and perhaps collapse, through hothouse forcing methods, while keeping them sufficiently flexible for the rapidly changing modern world. It is important to distinguish those functions which by their nature can only be advisory from those which should be executive, and to avoid the over-zealous tendency to change advisory bodies into executive ones (as has lately been apparent in the ILO and in certain private proposals concerning the Anglo-American Caribbean Commission) or to extend their field of operation beyond their assigned and natural scope. Agriculture, for instance, is governed so much by local conditions that it would be rash to try to direct it internationally, beyond some plan perhaps for the distribution and adjustment of crops, for improvements in methods, for research, and so on. On the other hand, projects like the Alcan (Alaska-Canadian) Highway could not have been carried out except through an authority with full administrative powers. The Chicago Conference on Civil Aviation (1944) ended in arrangements of very limited scope, yet long-range aviation could not be controlled, in the face of national competitive tendencies, except by some joint authority. Before the Second World War air control in Europe, which did not go far, practically bypassed the League's Organization for Communications and Transit under the separate Air Navigation Convention, and, outside that even, through agreements between governments and air companies. There is some excess of zeal also in the demand for some comprehensive international economic control. We have not yet come to that even within national economies, except in wartime and in totalitarian states.

I am not implying that the separate agencies, each with a function of its own, could or should work in watertight compartments. Co-ordination is clearly necessary, but it should come about when and in the measure in which it is needed. Here, again, one must think in terms of the varying nature of the case, and always keep in mind the need for flexibility. Within one and the same group of functions there might have to be co-ordination simply for technical reasons, or on a different level for the sake of a common policy. Rail, road, and air transport in Europe would need technical co-ordination in regard to timetables, etc., or a wider co-ordination if there is to be a distribution of passenger and freight traffic for the most economic performance—all of which might be done by some general body, perhaps on the lines of the United States Federal Commerce Commission. Again, the work of eventual agencies responsible for the control of minerals would have to be co-ordinated with those looking after possible synthetic substitutes. The next stage might be the co-ordination of several groups of agencies, where their activities meet or cross each other: For instance, the demands of transport agencies for rolling stock, ships, etc., may have to be co-ordinated with the demands of other services using the same materials and industries, perhaps by some body of the type of the inter-Allied war controls. A third stage would be to co-ordinate the working of administrative agencies with any international planning bodies. An international investment board or an international development commission could help to guide the growth of functional agencies into the most desirable channels, whether for the best use of existing resources or for ironing out cyclical trends, and so on. Co-ordination of such a general nature may in some cases amount almost to arbitration between functional agencies, and regional boards or councils like those of the Pan-American Union might be used for adjusting regional differences.[7] And insofar as it may be necessary to keep alive a general sense of our problem, i.e., to consider ends rather than means, and to keep a general watch over the policy of the various agencies, some representative body of the member countries could meet periodically for that wider supervisory purpose.

These are indeed the functions which are contemplated in Chapter IX of the Dumbarton Oaks scheme for the Economic and Social Council of the new international organization. This Council, and the General Assembly in which all states would have a voice, could discuss and ventilate general policies and be the vehicle of public opinion. It could not be given power to have an independent policy of its own, not only because this might turn out to be at odds with the policy of national parliaments or governments, but also because, as we have already said, the range of problems to be covered is so vast and conditions are so changeable that no general assembly could deal with them practically. The enunciation of general economic and social ends would fall properly within its scope, but conditions of performance must be left to the agencies responsible for each particular task. To try to mix the two could only do harm either to the reputation of Council and Assembly or to the effectiveness of the working agencies. In time we may realize the need for some central economic body; at the moment most countries are about to revise their economic organization from war- to peacetime needs, while such a forum, if it is to be of any use, will have to be given a substantial degree of authority by all the states. Any attempt to widen from the outset the formal authority

---

[7] The insistence of the U.S. administration that aid to the fifteen European countries grouped in the OEEC under the Marshall Plan should be based on a common plan and policy was a striking application of this point.

of the Economic and Social Council would inevitably result either in the clipping of its real powers or in the passing of its policy-making function into the hands of an "inner cabinet" of the big and wealthy states. If these states work together in the economic field the scope and authority of the Economic Council will grow naturally, but the Council could not make them co-operate no matter how much nominal authority we may try to give it.

The particular organization of international agencies must be left to be adapted to the character of each—whether we are dealing with administrative powers, with the representation of member governments, with internal organization and personnel, or, more especially, with matters of finance.[8] While advisory agencies would be dependent on continuous contributions from governments, executive agencies might acquire an autonomous budget of their own from the revenues of the service. Personnel will also have to be suited to the needs of the particular task; but, in general, conditions of service, security of tenure, pension rights, etc., must be such as to give recruits for an international civil service the possibility of devoting themselves to it unreservedly. The Middle East Supply Center, where the staff is predominantly technical and scientific, has shown what can be done for an area starved of technical efficiency, just as the secretariat of the League, which at first did not quite know what it was expected to do, showed that a capable and internationally minded staff can develop a fruitful initiative of its own. This kind of work will not grow and prosper unless we can build up gradually an international civil service inspired by opportunities for service to and through the world community and free from the pressure of nationalist influence. To that end the more developed countries must help to train personnel from the less developed countries, through some measure for edu-

[8] Mr. Chester Purves dealt with this aspect in detail in his conference paper, "Personnel and Finance" (*International Administration,* p. 12), and only a few general points are discussed here.

cational lend-lease, so that the proper choice by qualification should not result in a too one-sided choice by nationality.[9]

The question of the powers to be given to international agencies has been confused by the extreme attitude taken by many reformers, some of whom demand the "surrender" of national sovereignty, while other sections insist that nothing should be done which might in any way infringe it. There is no need for the first, and no international organization would be possible under the second view. Sovereignty is a legal concept, a status, which could be surrendered only to some world state or government. On the other hand, every arrangement between states by treaty, convention, or pact brings with it a voluntary limitation in the exercise of sovereignty within the range of the particular agreement. Joint international activities really amount to a pooling of certain sovereign rights; that is, for some clearly defined and usually limited purpose the participants agree to exercise their rights jointly. It would be the same whether those rights were exercised directly through a common council, like the present war controls, or indirectly through a common autonomous agency to which, for a particular task and for as long as it is performed, those rights would in effect be transferred. The nature and degree of the powers so transferred would clearly depend upon the nature of the task, and they might be increased or reduced as found by experience. If powers are transferred for a purpose which by common agreement is to be pursued no longer separately but jointly, the powers must clearly come in the first place from those who had formerly been engaged separately in that task.[10]

[9] The point is discussed in the paper "Reflections on the UNESCO Exchange of Persons Programme." This review of the UNESCO publication *Study Abroad,* Vol. 11, 1949, appeared in the *UNESCO International Social Science Bulletin,* Summer 1950.

[10] For example, in the 1937 Sugar Agreement the number of votes given to each country was arranged in proportion to the quotas of sugar exported or imported.

There is little sense, therefore, in another popular demand for full equality of all states in the control or performance of various international functions. It would already be a great advance if those states which own important resources were willing to place their use under some joint control, but they are hardly likely to do so if control were vested in a majority of "have-nots." Executive power will inevitably have to go together with capacity for performance. But any tendency to domination by the Great Powers would be reduced, and all countries would have some say in the directing of policy. Inequality in representation would be incidental to the task and would vary with it. Moreover, whatever the inequality in representation, the agency would serve a common interest and would give service to all participants in the measure of their practical needs. In that way less powerful and wealthy peoples would at least get a measure of real equality—not the voting equality of political democracy but the working equality of social democracy.

The pressure for social reform that is now felt everywhere is creating new claims and also new opportunities. It is changing utterly the relation of the individual to the state, and equally that of the national community to the world. There is so much of a common aspiration in all the many national plans that it calls for a joint effort in the most suitable practical way, leaving behind outgrown political divisions and means. The ways of national planning are often incompatible with the needs of other countries; they could only cause economic and social dislocation and all-round disruption for the supposed good of each of us separately. Our fine new social purpose cannot be conceived in discord and conflict. Conflict might bring full employment but not a full life, let alone a free life. Individual freedom within the state could not long survive international discord.

One might put it briefly that the historical function of the nineteenth century was to restrain the powers of arbitrary authority, and that led to the creation of "political man" and likewise of the "political nation." Our time is intent upon developing the social scope of authority, not by insulating the rights of the citizen but by co-ordinating his social claims with the powers of the authority responsible for satisfying them. Internationally, too, it is no longer a question of defining fixed relations between states in isolation but of merging their needs and relations actively—the workaday sense of the vague talk about the need to surrender some part of sovereignty. Even through the earlier hesitant experiments in international action one can see a continuous evolution—an evolution closely related to the perennial changes in national life. There is a clear thread of progress to be discerned in the advance from fitful royal gatherings to regular political conferences, and from these, through the working of the technical factor, to international unions and bureaus. With rare exceptions, in the past these agencies have in the main had the character of secretariats, policy and execution being outside their scope; that was still true of the League secretariat and even of the ILO. In this era of planning the inevitable next step is to move on from the secretarial to the executive stage, to create wherever needed international agencies with administrative functions and powers of their own. Such an advance is bound to be experimental; therefore there is everything to be said for dealing with each task separately. The difficulties of one need not thus embarrass the others; and especially, by tying up each international strand functionally, we shall avoid being hampered by differences in the economic and social organization and outlook of the participants. There will be ample opportunity for co-ordinating the several activities as and when the need arises. One might add that the working, and especially the co-ordination, of functional activities would build up not only sectors of international administration but gradually also a body of international administrative law, which in the end might do more toward unifying the ways of the world than attempts at codifying abstract juridical rules and principles. International society will acquire a living body not by our pledging each other in solemn pacts and charters but by our working together in the humble tasks of everyday life.[11]

Postscript

It was suggested in discussion that the judiciary of the new international organization should be given a more important role—a very desirable goal. But, first, a judiciary is only one of the organs of a comprehensive political system. Its authority is derivative; it cannot stand above and go beyond that of the general system. Second, the judiciary can only interpret existing law and agreed rules of conduct; but there is no adequate body of international law, while the international field is too new and loose and varied, and too uncertain, for a system of equity. And any attempt to start with a set and codified law—if the judiciary is careful of legal forms, as judges have to be—may actually hold up practical advances; this has often been the effect of constitutional interpretations by the United States Supreme Court.

One can appreciate the wish to move forward boldly; but I think it true to say in regard to progress within our own states that it has not been a case of institutional and constitutional changes bringing about practical advances, but rather of their having marked the consolidation of advances which have gradually become accepted practice.

---

[11] It has been said that Benjamin Franklin did more toward unifying the country by creating a national postal service than did constitutional rules.

III
THE FUNCTIONAL
APPROACH
AND FEDERALISM

The Functional
Approach to
World Organization

It seems to be the fate of all periods of transition that reformers are more ready to fight over a doctrine than to pull together on a problem. At this stage I only ask to be given credit for the claim that I do not represent a doctrine or a dogma; I represent an anxiety. At home when we want change or reform we state our objectives in such terms that all may see how we propose to attain them. When it comes to the international world, where we are faced with old and stubborn habits of mind and feeling and political dogma, where the change we have in mind must close one of the heavy tomes of history and open up a new one, it seems that nothing will do but the perfect goal and winged results.

When we compare the general mood of 1919, when everybody

The argument between those who believe that the states of Europe, and of the world, could and should be linked together in a federation and those who doubt whether that is possible or indeed desirable became sharper in 1948, the year which saw the first meeting of the Consultative Assembly of the Council of Europe. This paper was read at a private meeting of members of the Royal Institute of International Affairs on March 4, 1948, and was printed in *International Affairs* for July 1948.

was eager to get back to the old order of things, with the mood of 1948, only one generation later, when the need for an active international society is almost universally taken for granted—then we are surely justified in regarding the change as progress indeed. For without such a change in outlook all schemes for international peace, as in past centuries, would remain but noble dreams. Yet even with this change present schemes may likewise remain noble dreams if they are beyond the reach of the ways and means of practical everyday government. "Government is a practical thing," Burke wrote to the sheriffs of Bristol, and one should beware of elaborating political forms "for the gratification of visionaries." Vagueness in this difficult transition will merely produce vagueness in popular sentiment. If the new popular receptiveness to the idea of international organization is to ripen into an informed public opinion, it must now be fed with a diet of hard facts and with proposals that are visibly practicable, so that it may know how to press and support governments in the pursuit of a positive international policy. The task of experts in this field, whether individuals or groups, is to pass now beyond fine appeals and ideal formulas. There has already been too much pleading and too little thinking. How otherwise explain why, with such broad good will and a sense of urgency, so little has been fulfilled?

The general outlook is promising. When we come to examine present trends more closely two stand out above all—the trend for national self-government and the trend for radical social change. The intensity of the two trends varies in different parts of the world, but everywhere they tend to merge into one political current. Even in Europe, where there is little room left for new state-making, the transformation of society is taking place on a national basis; while in the Middle East, in Southeast Asia, in Africa, and elsewhere, the new states are an expression of social revolution as much as of political revolution.

From the international point of view there is a danger in this.

Such social nationalism, or national socialism, is actually bringing about a regression. The modern political trend has led increasingly to the splitting up of the world into independent states. The idea of national self-government, the guiding principle of the peace settlement of 1919, is still strongly at work in the Middle East, in Southeast Asia, and in Africa; while at the same time modern economic life, with its extensive division of labor, has tended to weld peoples and countries socially together. It is that living unity which is in danger of being bruised and battered by the new conception of the planned welfare state. It is not my business to discuss whether this trend is desirable or inevitable, but merely to establish that these are the conditions from which our international house-building has to start. We are favored by the need and the habit of material co-operation; we are hampered by the general clinging to political segregation. How to reconcile these two trends, both of them natural and both of them active, is the main problem for political invention at this juncture of history.

Speaking broadly, ideas and schemes for international organization can be considered under one of three categories: (1) a general and fairly loose association, like the League of Nations and the United Nations, (2) a federal union, and (3) a system of functional arrangements. Whatever our personal inclinations, we have to look at these alternatives against the conditions of the time, and with the ultimate end of international government in mind.

Both the League of Nations and the United Nations, as their names imply, have been based upon national separateness. They could be taken as loose associations for certain specified and limited joint ends, or as clubs making joint action easier if needed and if approved according to their constitutional provisions. But the United Nations cannot, and neither could the League, prescribe action to its member states, much less take action on its own authority.

Our short but tense experience since the creation of the United Nations has shown that such a loose arrangement is inadequate in its scope and uncertain in its working. Hence, no doubt, the widespread interest in the federal idea in a variety of forms. Federalism is one of the great inventions of political theory. It came to us from the New World and has been adopted in a number of places, especially in newer political groupings. It has served admirably where a number of adjacent and related provinces or countries, while retaining a substantial separate identity, wanted to join together for some important common purpose. Federation has been the political equivalent of a company with limited liability. Habitually a federal union rests upon a number of similar elements—a degree of close kinship or historical relationship, and a will to unity—but with them also a clear intent by the parts to manage many of their social affairs separately. How does all this apply to the international scene?

We have been presented with a choice of proposals for international federation. Some advocate, variously and vaguely, European federation or Western federation or democratic federation; others, more ambitiously, world federation. The fact that there are so many differing and overlapping proposals shows that they are not impelled by any inherent force of kinship or sense of unity into the suggested groupings. Any of them may be desirable, but we have no proof that any of them is desired. There is no evidence of the will to unite. Indeed most of these ideas, even that for European federation, have been pressed upon peoples who themselves have shown no lively signs of wishing to take the initiative. Alternatively, they have been urged to federate so as to be better able to stand up to other antagonistic political groupings. The advice may be sound, but it is an argument for a new nationalism, not for a new internationalism. Hitherto federation has indeed merely created a new and larger political unit which in the process did bring peace within the group, but it has not been proved that its creation necessarily contributed also to peace between it and other groups.

The prospect of two powerful federations, for instance, facing each other across Europe, is not a comforting one. It would not check the more disturbing of the present general trends, that toward political division; it would change the dimensions of nationalism but not its nature.

But let us for the sake of argument take the most hopeful view as to the will of the states to unite in wider political units, and leave aside for the moment the negative kind of peace that this would represent. The main question is really this—whether some kind of international federation under present conditions would strengthen the trend toward the social integration of international life, making of it a general and positive foundation for peace. A federation comes into being for certain specific ends; a federation unites, but it also restricts. It rests on a rigid division of powers and functions between territorial authorities which formally have equal status, and that division is usually and necessarily laid down in a written constitution, provided with an armory of safeguards against its being easily tampered with. In a volume of essays on federal planning, Professor Wheare grants that federal government is by its nature conservative and legalistic.[1] Every attempt to give the central government some new function or power has to knock long at the massive and rusty gates of the constitution. The efforts of the Canadian government to change the fiscal arrangements of the federation have been blocked so far, in spite of long discussion and patent need. In Australia repeated efforts for concerted economic and social action have been similarly balked, and the recent decision to nationalize the banking system shook the political structure and temper of the country.[2] Even in such a dynamic country as the United States the sin of unconstitutionality has often bedev-

[1] P. Ransome, ed., *Studies in Federal Planning* (London, Macmillan, 1943).

[2] In 1948 the Australian Labour government introduced a bill which was brought before the high court, to be finally defeated on constitutional grounds in the Privy Council. The Labour government went out of office in 1949, and the bill has not since been re-introduced.

iled efforts at social reform—such as the prohibition of child labor in factories—and killed or maimed most of the original New Deal measures. The now universally admired and imitated TVA experiment had to sustain some forty legal suits or more on grounds of unconstitutionality before it was allowed to settle down to its great work.

It is curious how those who urge the use of the federal idea internationally have neglected this central characteristic of its working. Jefferson, politically wise beyond a man's measure, foresaw the dangers of a rigid constitution and wished to provide for its periodical revision every ten years. Such a provision, for just such a term, was part of the old Austro-Hungarian federal arrangement, the so-called *Ausgleich,* with the result that every term became a crisis which brought with it a threat of dissolution —causing the irrepressible Viennese wits to speak of it as *"Monarchie auf Kündigung."* And yet such an entrenched restraint is not unreasonable. New functions and new powers granted to the supposedly co-equal central authority, however beneficent the social purpose for which they are claimed, must have politically a cumulative effect; and a sufficient number of such additions would before long permanently change the balance upon which any federation is established. As Professor Alexander Brady points out, it took almost twenty years of difficult negotiations to find a basis for the federation of Australia, and the reluctance to see it changed is therefore understandable.[3] To come into being at all an international federation would have to start with a very narrow common denominator and with very rigid arrangements as to form and functions, and the reluctance to allow these to be lightly disturbed would be correspondingly all the greater.

In an international federation every adaptation, every amendment would have to run the gauntlet of jealous argument between

[3] "Dominion Nationalism and the Commonwealth," *Canadian Journal of Economics and Political Science,* February 1944, p. 9.

countries newly come together and differing in their political background. Even in agreed common matters the pace can only be that of the slowest member of the group; issues which divide deeply must be shunned. But in our time conditions, needs, and problems are apt to change rapidly. Either the constitution would have to be continuously adapted or the difficulty of such adaptation would hobble the life and government of the federation. Can such a rigid instrument then be made to fit the present revolutionary mood which, whatever we may think of it, is surging throughout the world? People have been puzzled that the most revolutionary of all governments—one whose ideology stands for world unity and the withering away of the state—has on every possible occasion and at the United Nations insisted on the strict observance of national sovereignty. The explanation can be found in a recent article on sovereignty by Professor I. D. Levin, a leading Soviet jurist, who uses the very argument adumbrated above: that in a revolutionary situation any and every people must be free to transform its social organization as it wills, without external interference or complications.[4] Professor Levin is obviously right in assuming that this would not be possible under some rigid and comprehensive form of political association. If a federal house cannot be half free and half slave, neither can it be half capitalist and half communist. Every attempt at some fundamental change in one part would put in jeopardy the continuance of the whole; for the alternatives would appear to the legalists as disruption and to the reformers as stagnation.

A federal system has many virtues. But in form and working it is a combination of rigidities: rigid in its framework, whether geographical or ideological; rigid in its constitution, which has to be formal and unchallenged; rigid in its general life, because of the

---

[4] "Problema suverenteta v ustave OON" ("The Problem of Sovereignty in the U.N. Statute"), *Sovetskoe Gosudarstvo i Pravo* (Moscow), No. 1, 1947, pp. 17–29.

limits and obstacles the constitution places in the path of fresh common action. If under present conditions of political nationalism an international federation would be difficult to achieve, under present conditions of social revolution it would be even more difficult to maintain. Its only prospect would be either to limit it to the lowest common denominator as regards membership—such as the Benelux or a Scandinavian group—or to restrict it to the lowest common denominator as regards federal functions and powers. And if a dynamic federal grouping is not possible, a federal grouping so limited in membership or so restricted in its activities would be meaningless as a contribution to the problem of world unity.

The main central functions of federations have always been common defense and foreign policy. These indeed, with a common budget for their purpose, Mr. Lionel Curtis considers sufficient to start the world federal arrangement which he has advocated so eloquently and devotedly. But is this not again neglecting the historical perspective? Not only are the number of functions which need joint action apt to change; their character is apt to change even more rapidly. A hundred or even fifty years ago, defense and foreign policy absorbed only a limited part of the total life of the community. Now between them they control material resources and the organization of industry, manpower and training, and even education and opinion, and sweeping controls of trade as of fiscal and financial policy.

Federation, to sum up, was born in times of enthusiasm for formal constitutions; now we are in a pragmatic mood that scorns rigid bonds and restrictions. Federalism was meant to put into the hands of central authority the least possible functions of common life; now the run of political life can only mean leaving in the hands of the individual authority the least possible functions of local life. It was born when in general the scope of government was limited, whereas now we live feverishly and somewhat precariously under limitless planning and controls. If a world union were to try to do all those things for political security and for social security which present trends demand—and inevitably they would have to be done through the instrument of a central authority—it would all end in the paradox that the federal idea would be proclaimed only to be stripped of all the meaning and virtue of a federation.

Thus to expose the difficulties of the federal idea does not come from any inclination to be destructive. It is rather the outcome of a conviction that in this stubborn international field we cannot hope to make progress by propounding schemes with a pleasant symmetry without regard to the rough and shifty terrain on which they have to be grounded. In looking at the federal idea against present conditions and needs, I have really been trying to draw attention to the sociological framework within which any effort toward international government would have to work. Shaped as it is both by the will for national distinctness and by the need for social integration, that framework would be difficult to construct simply by changing the dimensions of our traditional political instruments. We must rather look for a new political device, and the device best suited to construct that framework out of the present historical material would seem to be the functional idea—not new as an invention but new in its application.

The functional approach has indeed been used a great deal even in established federations—in particular very successfully in America by the New Deal, with the TVA scheme as its outstanding example. Two circumstantial points arise here. If, it may be argued, existing federations have been able to carry through great reforms in this way, does not this break the argument that the federal idea would prove a drag to international social action? Though plausible at first sight, the point does not stand up to closer examination. Existing federations can sometimes get around formal federal divisions only because they are old-established federations. Generations of common life and experience have welded their component parts into a society with a common outlook, with common problems expressed in the programs of national parties. In their case a common central government has come to be taken for granted, with state or provincial governments more on the level of local administrative bodies. The significant exception of Quebec within the Canadian federation proves indeed the need for such common background. In most cases the problem, therefore, was not so much a matter of creating a common policy as of consolidating a line of similar or identical policies. Yet in times of crisis even in such old-established federations the joint national activities were expanded not by changing constitutional arrangements but rather by circumventing them. In no case has there been any deliberate change in the formal hierarchy of power. Federal governments have simply taken upon themselves many new tasks, with tacit national consent, and in that way acquired new powers by functional accretion, not by constitutional revision. In the United States the only attempt at constitutional change during Roosevelt's presidency—to increase the membership of the federal Supreme Court—was also the only issue on which he was utterly defeated; and yet its effect would have been relatively marginal compared with the revolutionary impact of the New Deal as a whole.

America has used the functional approach also in starting new lines of association with neighboring states, not only in the close wartime arrangements with Canada, a matter of expediency, but in permanent measures. The Alcan Highway has created a strip of international administration running from the United States through Canada to Alaska; the arrangement with Mexico for the development of the Rio Grande has turned a river frontier into a joint enterprise of common benefit; and Pan-American developments are likely to follow the same line. Experiments such as these have a particular lesson for the wider international problem. There is a simple lesson in the sheer fact that they can be made; but there is a more significant lesson in that the United States found it easier to complete the Alcan arrangement with Canada and the Rio Grande arrangement with Mexico than to set in motion its own TVA scheme. The first two were made with sovereign countries prepared to pool their resources and to relinquish that part of their sovereignty necessary for a specific joint functional undertaking. The TVA experiment affected federal units which were reluctant to part with any of their share of power and which therefore tried hard to maintain the original balance laid down in the federal Constitution.

A more extreme example was the insistence of the Australian government, against American reluctance, on the inclusion in the San Francisco Charter (1945) of some form of international undertaking to work for "full employment"—an "obligation" meant to give the Australian government the right to take internal social action which would otherwise be beyond its constitutional powers. That was indeed a striking and novel way of overcoming federal obstructions by courting international obligations. (The incident also illustrated how the content of foreign policy is changing.) In the United States and other federations, necessary nation-wide action has been possible in the face of constitutional obstacles because there existed an old and live sense of national unity. A new international federation would have no such ingrained sense of unity, and constitutional barriers would obstruct all the more impassably at every corner. And as we have seen, even those old federations have at times found it easier to make functional arrangements with foreign states than within their own community.

The truth is that by its very nature the constitutional approach emphasizes the individual index of power; the functional approach emphasizes the common index of need. Very many such needs cut across national boundaries; not a few are universal, and an effective beginning for building up an international community of interest could be made by setting up joint agencies for dealing with these common needs. And this is both an urgent and an opportune moment for such positive steps in international government. The emergence of so many new national states will complicate politically our difficulties, but socially this multiplication might be put to the service of international unification. For if these new and mostly undeveloped states are to achieve a healthy social foundation for their political independence they will need many things which are beyond their means and experience; and, as in the case of the Marshall Plan, such needs could be used deliberately and insistently to set up lines for joint international action.

The universal popular demand for social security could likewise be turned into a channel for international unity. Everywhere the new nationalism is a peculiarly social nationalism. As in the nineteenth century, many a people wants to have its own national house, but unlike the earlier nationalism it is especially intent upon a new form of social life within that house. There is much to be said for one solid international block of flats, but as long as people choose to live in detached national houses we could at least go a long way toward establishing a sense of community by supplying them with joint social and other services. Only in some such way is there any prospect, for instance, of mending the breach in the political unity of the Indian continent and of restoring there an awareness of the unity of natural common interests; whereas any suggestion for political reunion between India and Pakistan would make even proposals for practical common action suspect. Again, this seems the only possible hope of mending the division between Arabs and Jews and, indeed, of building some true unity among the Arab countries themselves, along the path so admirably mapped out by the Middle East Supply Center during the Second World War. In the Danubian region, in spite of much ideological fraternizing, a mere reference by the Bulgarian Communist leader, M. Dimitrov, to a federal link-up at once brought a rebuke from Moscow and little response from his neighbors; but those same countries are apparently working on a scheme for a Danube Valley Authority.

Much could be learned from an examination of the structure and working of the wartime functional arrangements, or of the work of the International Labor Organization in giving a common direction to policies of social improvement without encroaching on state sovereignty. The French, Belgian, and British governments are now working out lines of co-operation for their African territories, ranging from sanitation, irrigation, and soil conservation to the common use of communications and other services, with a view to co-ordinating economic, educational, and administrative policies.[5]

It is not only in the fields of government and economics that the functional approach can bring relief. In a noteworthy sermon the Archbishop of Canterbury boldly admitted that all schemes of reunion between the English churches had failed because, he insisted, they had tried a doctrinal reunion. He called for a different, a more humble but practical approach through the exchange of ministers and pulpits. "It is because I fear stalemate," said Dr. Fisher, "that I venture to throw out this suggestion—Can we grow to full communion with each other before we write a constitution?"[6] The evolution of the Flemish problem in Belgium is also instructive. During the First World War the political separatist movement created a bitter reaction in the country and almost led to civil strife. Since then, by gradual, quiet changes, the Flem-

---

[5] The Commission for Technical Co-operation South of the Sahara was established in 1950 and has the support of eight governments (Ghana, Liberia, Rhodesia and Nyasaland, Union of South Africa, Belgium, France, Portugal, and the United Kingdom). There are six technical bodies acting under its auspices as well as other technical bureaus and committees dealing with matters of rural welfare, soil utilization, tsetse fly, etc., etc. See the publication of the Commission, *Inter-African Scientific and Technical Co-operation, 1948–1955.*

[6] Sermon by Dr. Geoffrey Fisher, November 3, 1946, before the University of Cambridge; reported in *The Times* (London), November 4, 1946.

ings have obtained complete autonomy in education—the University of Ghent is now completely Flemish and that of Liège completely French—and almost as wide autonomy in the administration of the Flemish area. In addition, there has grown a close cultural association between the Belgian Flemings and Dutch institutions and activities. No constitutional provision has so far legalized this evolution, while on the other hand talk of political separation has died out among the Flemings.

Earlier in this essay I pointed out, as one proof of the weakness of the federal idea, the many varieties of schemes competing for public support. There are as many, if not more, schemes for functional experiment. Does that not show a similar fragility of conception? Perhaps nothing brings out more clearly than this question how different in essence is the federalist from the functional approach. Under the federal idea the several schemes are mutually exclusive: A state could not be in both a European and a Commonwealth federation, or in both a European and some general democratic federation. Functional schemes, on the other hand, are at best complementary, each helping the others; at worst, they remain independent of each other. Any such scheme can be started at any time, whether the others are accepted or not, and any one may live and prosper even if others fail and are abandoned. In our politically ever-changing times, functional arrangements have the invaluable virtue of autonomous existence and likewise of autonomous development. A scheme started originally by a few countries for transport, for example, could later be broadened to include new members or reduced to let reluctant ones drop out. Moreover, such schemes can vary in their membership; countries can take part only in activities in which they have an interest, not in others, whereas in any political union such a divided choice would obviously not be tolerable. Functional "neutrality" is possible; political "neutrality" is not. The requirements of an international federal authority for the conduct, for instance, of a common foreign policy would always have to be a matter of political bargaining. The requirements of a functional authority for the needs of the clear-cut task entrusted to it—for example, in charge of oil or aviation—would at any given time be a matter of factual audit.

These characteristics of the functional approach therefore can help to mitigate the obstinate problem of equal sovereignty. Under this idea it is not a matter of surrendering sovereignty but merely of pooling as much of it as may be needed for the joint performance of a particular task. Under such practical arrangements governments do not need, as in political schemes, to safeguard their right to equal voting, but can allow a special position to those countries with a particular responsibility for the task concerned—so long as the service is performed for the benefit of all. All this is in keeping with the whole trend of modern government. Twentieth-century government means less a division of powers than an integration of functions. Administration and administrative law are its characteristic tools, and such functional arrangements would simply mean giving international range to administrative organs and jurisdiction, in accordance with the nature of each task. They would also be in harmony with the social philosophy of our time. As a former head of the FAO said of his particular responsibility: "Here in this world food plan we have the means whereby the nations could begin to co-operate on something which would do none of them harm and do all of them good." Insofar as governments have only the welfare of their own peoples at heart there can be no reason why they should not allow such organizations to go to work; and if the organizations are successful and their number grows, world government will gradually evolve through their performance. From the point of view of normal daily life, to quote the late Professor Hobhouse, "the life of a community may be regarded as the sum of the functions performed by its members"; conversely, the performance of a number of common functions is the way to create a normal community. If one were to visualize a map of the world designed to show international economic and social activities, it would appear as an intricate web of interests and relations, crossing and re-crossing political divisions—not a sullen map of isolated states but a map pulsating with the beneficent intercourse of everyday life. And it is this which is the natural basis for international organization. The task is to bring that map, which is already functioning as a reality, under the control of some form of joint international agencies. Then the political dividing lines would in time be overlaid and blurred by that web of joint relations and administrations.

A close association of states can be either comprehensive or selective. Clearly the first is the ideal—all countries working together for the common good. But if it cannot be comprehensive, if it has to be selective, it is better that it be selective on lines of common activities rather than of exclusive groups. Whereas any one country may join a particular activity, a set group cannot help being exclusive; and, in the words of Dr. Johnson, "such is the disposition of man, that whatever makes a distinction creates rivalry." Seen in this light, the functional approach implies not merely a change of political device but a change of political outlook. It should help to shift the emphasis from political issues which divide to those social issues in which the interests of the nations are plainly akin and collective; to shift the emphasis from power to problems and purpose.

In all societies there are to be found both harmonies and disharmonies. It is largely within our choice which we pick out and further. Since the end of the Second World War we have had many a brutal illustration of this truth at peace conferences and at meetings of the United Nations, at which the new international life was supposed to be born. Therefore we must begin anew, with a clear sense that the nations can be bound together into a world community only if we link them up by what unites, not by what divides. In the second place, ways and means to that end must be fitted to the purpose in hand. They have to be adequate, but they also must be relevant; and if they are to be relevant they must start from the conditions which we find around us. They must avoid reaction but also avoid Utopia. We can ask our fellowmen to look beyond the national state; we cannot expect them to feel themselves at once members of a world state. During his first months as President, Jefferson wrote to a friend that he realized how short he would fall of achieving all that reason and experience justified. But "when we reflect how difficult it is to move or inflect the great machine of society, how impossible to advance the notions of a whole people suddenly to ideal right, we see the wisdom of Solon's remark, that no more good must be attempted than the nation can bear."[7]

In our case, and in our time, what the nations can bear varies according to the nature of the load. Taken by and large, they seem as yet unable to bear much interference with their political independence, but they can bear quite a lot of it when it comes to practical economic and social action.[8] The distinction gives a first guiding line for peaceful international action. The next question is how such economic and social action should be organized so as to lead the nations toward international community and international government. In our own countries we are becoming accus-

[7] Andrew A. Lipscomb and Albert E. Berch, eds., *The Writings of Thomas Jefferson* (Washington, 1903–4), Vol. 10, p. 256.

[8] The new states, politically tangled up in aggressively "uncommitted" groups and leagues, have shown themselves eager to join the U.N.'s special agencies and other such bodies, "because the balance of considerations is in favor of such participation," and they have come to look upon it "as an international asset and a strengthening of their position in the world." In spite of their extreme sensitiveness the new states have shown little mistrust of such bodies, "even where the activities of the international organization within the state's territory is concerned." (Benjamin Akzin, "New States and International Organizations" [Paris, UNESCO, 1955], pp. 170–72.)

tomed to putting nearly all such action into the hands of the central government. Are we ready to follow the same course in the international sphere? If we are, a federation, with its restrictive constitutional machinery, would hardly be the proper instrument. A federation leaving those social and economic activities in the hands of its national members would, in this respect, be little more than a replica of the United Nations. If, on the other hand, those activities were to be entrusted to a central international authority, with effective powers and means, that authority will be no less than a full-fledged world government. The larger social and economic tasks will, of necessity, have to be performed jointly and to be controlled centrally. The true choice, therefore, is not between the present competitive nationalisms and a lame international federation; the choice is between a full-fledged and comprehensive world government and equally full-fledged but specific and separate functional agencies.

Functional
Federalism

Federalists always present the United States as living proof that
this is the way to unite the countries of Europe and of the world.
I have therefore pointed out, as in the preceding essay, that when
great changes have to be undertaken, such as the complex of reforms known as the New Deal, it has been found necessary even in
federations to use a functional approach rather than attempt constitutional amendments. In reply, M. Chiti-Batelli argues that if
functional arrangements have been possible in America, it is precisely because they have worked *within* a federal system.

This is an important point. Have functional arrangements
worked only under the protection of a federal umbrella, and have
federal arrangements helped the working of functional activities?
Fortunately we can get closer to the issue by coming down to concrete experience. For the past century or so a large and growing

In *Common Cause* for April 1950 (the Journal of the Committee to
Frame a World Constitution, Chicago), M. Andrea Chiti-Batelli examined
certain aspects of what he called functional federalism, and in doing so
took issue with my argument that a federal system is not suited to the
intense kind of government which is evolving in our present welfare or
service state. The editors of *Common Cause* with great courtesy invited
me to comment on M. Chiti-Batelli's own view, and published the reply
in their journal in November 1950.

number of international arrangements—such as the International Postal Union, the wartime Combined Boards, the many defense and industrial arrangements between the United States and Canada, and many others—have been set up and have worked well without reference to any common political authority. That is the positive side. But there is also much evidence that the existence of a federal constitution, with its fixed division of attributions and powers, has stood in the way of practical functional developments.

The needs of the war were bound to lead everywhere to an increase in central functions and controls, but the reaction in existing federations was swift and general. In Canada, as in Australia and Switzerland, there has been repeated and growing opposition to reforms or new common activities, however desirable, because the component units are afraid that any new common activity would upset the established constitutional balance of power in favor of the central authority. All this may seem to play rather one-sidedly on the difficulties that spring from federal arrangements. Do not the trials of the Schuman Plan (for the European Coal and Steel Community) show that there are plenty of difficulties also in the functional idea? Obviously there are, but that does not make the federal prospect any easier. If people will not accept such limited international action why assume that the wider idea will be more welcome? Would the chances of the Schuman Plan be improved if its initiator were to say, "Let us federate first"? Or again, looking at the tribulations of the United Nations scheme for the international control of atomic energy (as proposed by America under the so-called Baruch Plan), would anyone care to suggest that it would be easier to get the U.S.S.R. to join a world federation first? A world federation without the U.S.S.R., on the other hand, would not solve the atomic problem; it would leave it almost where it stands now.

This obvious fact seems to reveal the true core of the international problem, as it also reveals why clinging to a set political formula, in the face of the increasing pressure of practical needs, has produced among federalists a strange dialectical confusion. M. Chiti-Batelli was aware of this and more than justified in complaining of it. We shall never get a public opinion that can judge an idea intelligently if the makers of the idea do not care what political ingredients they mix together as long as they can retain the original label. Take this instance from a recent publication by a well-known European federalist, M. Denis de Rougemont: In a pamphlet, *The Way of Federalism,* he lays down six "governing principles" as a way to federation, the last of which he describes as follows:

> I foresee European federation growing slowly, in many different places and in many different ways. Here, an economic agreement, there, a cultural affinity. In one area two churches with similar beliefs will share communion; in another a group of small states will form a customs union. And, above all, private individuals will create, little by little, a series of networks for the exchange of ideas. All this is useful, and all this, seemingly so dispersed, often so ineffective, will gradually build up complex structures, marking in outline the skeleton and blood vessels of what will be one day the body of the United States of Europe.[1]

And he adds for good measure that a federation is formed "not by working from the center outward, or through the medium of governments"! This bewildering political concoction almost tempts one to say, paraphrasing Gilbert and Sullivan, that "when everything is federal, then nothing's federation." It bears, of course, no relation whatever to anything that has been understood by students as federation or to any of the ways in which existing federations have actually come about.

The obvious and elementary distinction between the federal and

[1] "Federal Union" (London, 1950), p. 13.

the functional idea was put clearly by M. H. M. Lange, the Norwegian Minister for External Affairs, in an article he wrote in
April 1950: "In the Strasbourg Assembly there emerged in the
course of last summer's debate two distinct schools of thought."
One group favored "what might be termed the constitutional, or the
federal, approach to the problem. They wanted to start with a
draft constitution for the United States of Europe." The other
group favored "what might be termed the functional approach.
They wanted to take up concrete projects for practical co-
operation in various fields and evolve such intra-European machinery as would be necessary to carry out the projects."[2] What
can the ordinary citizen be expected to think when he sees Winston
Churchill, no mean hand at politics or words, first raise the flag of
European union; then say at Strasbourg in 1948 that he could
accept union but not federation; and, finally, in 1950 let his Conservative followers join Labour delegates at the Strasbourg Consultative Assembly in declaring that no British government could
accept any arrangement, such as the Schuman Plan, which would
place decisions in important economic fields in the hands of a
supra-national authority?

One of the chief British supporters of federal union, Lord Layton (a vice-president of the Strasbourg Consultative Assembly),
has now had to confess that the movement has lost ground since
the first meeting of the Assembly, because, he admitted, British
opinion is not ready to accept a comprehensive political union,
though ready to relinquish some sovereign rights for certain clearly
defined and limited ends.[3] That is indeed the point which has
given rise to this discussion. Now the admission of Lord Layton
emboldens me to go a step further and say not only that federal
constitutions are apt to be a hindrance to practical action, but that
the mere advocacy of the idea itself may have the same effect. The

[2] "European Union: False Hopes and Realities," *Foreign Affairs,* April
1950, p. 448.
[3] Reported in the *Manchester Guardian,* January 28, 1950.

Indian Prime Minister said not long ago that India and Pakistan could and should do quite a number of things together, but what would have been Pakistan's response if Pandit Nehru had suggested political federation as a necessary preliminary to such practical co-operation?

When he took office last year the Australian Prime Minister, Mr. Menzies, remarked that "now that all legal attributes of the independence of British nations have been settled, it would be well to concentrate on matters of substance" and co-ordinate the production and distribution of food and raw materials for the benefit of the Commonwealth as a whole.[4] But it is the removal of political bonds which has transformed the old and strained British Empire into a co-operative Commonwealth. Any attempt to create new political ties would certainly cause the several parts of the Commonwealth to draw back; they would also be more reluctant to allow the growth of common activities if they were bound by a formal constitution to a central political authority.[5] The prototype of the newer functional conception is the TVA. It is true, as is often argued, that the TVA came into being within an existing federal system, but it is as often overlooked that because of that system the TVA had to meet some forty legal attacks on constitutional grounds before it could begin working properly. And what would have been the chances of its coming into being at all if the seven states concerned had been asked first to sink their separate statehood into one new political unit? Why do states' rights and regional claims, after almost two centuries of unity, still play an insistent and obstructive part in America's everyday life if the federal bond, as is assumed, is the best way of breaking down communal divisions?

But in any case, as far as the wider world problem is concerned,

[4] Reported in *The Times* (London), December 13, 1949.
[5] See David Mitrany, "Functional Co-operation in the Commonwealth," in *British Commonwealth: A Family of Nations,* ed., Sir Drummond Shiels; new edition (London, Odhams, 1959).

the argument whether the New Deal won out because of or in spite of the existence of a federal constitution is neither here nor there. The problem of our time is how to persuade the large number of sovereign states spread over the world to act together under present conditions. The true point for comparison, therefore, is not that thirteen American colonies were induced to federate some 160 years ago, but whether if the forty-eight states had developed as fully separate political and economic units they could be induced to federate *now*. Moreover, and still more important, could they be induced to federate on the very different basis which the present social climate demands? Federation was achieved in America when government did little and was intended to do no more. Now we are being swept forward by a revolutionary social current which demands continuous and increasing action by central governments and forces all the countries of the world to use new ways of economic and social planning—a process that is bound to turn each country into a tighter and more rigid separate unit unless by some means it can be diverted promptly and effectively into channels of international planning and action.

Therefore the problem is not merely one of somehow linking together a large number of states with different histories and outlook and in greatly varying stages of economic and social development. It is especially the problem of how to link them together in such a way that the new international authority, whatever its form, should be able to do as freely and intensively what is now being done nationally in the way of economic and social planning. The federal idea thus faces an impossible dilemma, which explains the confusion in the minds of some of its protagonists. M. Chiti-Batelli denounces this confusion, yet he would have to acquit it of theoretical sin if he had traced it to its sociological source. In Europe, and all the more so in the wider world, federal union could be secured, if at all, only by an extreme constriction of the powers and functions allotted to the central authority. On the other hand, only intensive and uniform action through some common authority can fulfill the social tasks of our time.

The real choice is clearly not between federation and some other and looser political form; the real choice is between social performance through national action and social performance through international planning and action. Nothing would be more fatal to the growth of a true international society than a federal system with a high-sounding title but with a central authority severely restricted in its powers and functions and with its progress checked by a rigid federal constitution. The supporters of the federal idea have been so hypnotized by the attractions of its form that they have neglected to study its present performance in existing federations, and these are all national federations. Much less have they examined whether the conditions of passive government under which these national federations came into being bear comparison with the conditions of intense governmental activity in which the host of heterogeneous states would have to be joined together now.

The Prospect of European Integration: Federal or Functional

On the day the Consultative Assembly was to meet at Strasbourg for the first time, the *Manchester Guardian* welcomed it in a somewhat questioning editorial. It was altogether a "strange experiment. Perhaps never before has an old aspiration seen the light so utterly unprepared for facing the world." That might be said now of many plans, and even acts, which have gone into the effort for European union. The pains taken to study its problems have been trifling compared with the vast propagandist pressure. The most assertive pleas have come from the federalists, and they have supported it often by pointing to the success of the American federation. That federation was born in much simpler conditions than those facing twentieth-century Europe; and yet with what searching inquiry did Madison and Hamilton and Jay argue their case in the eighty-six papers of *The Federalist,* and with what a straight and almost humble appeal to the *minds* of the electors! If the effort to understand be tedious and irksome, Hamilton wrote in the fif-

This paper appeared in the *Journal of Common Market Studies* (Oxford), December 1965.

teenth paper, "you will recollect, that you are in quest of information on a subject the most momentous which can engage the attention of a free people; that the field through which you have to travel is in itself spacious; and that the difficulties of the journey have been unnecessarily increased by the mazes with which sophistry has beset the way."

In our case two recent writers, with a sympathy for the idea, have commented on the difficulties laid for the student-traveler through the "spacious field" of European union. Mrs. Miriam Camps comments that "the line between what is actually happening today and what is hoped will be happening tomorrow is frequently obscured by those people who have been most closely involved in the 'making of Europe' "; partly it may have been due to enthusiasm, but in part "a deliberate tactic" designed "to generate the support that success, or complete confidence in success, attracts." In a lecture he gave in London, in December 1964 (printed in the review *World Today*), the head of the EEC Commission, Dr. Walter Hallstein, simply told his hearers that "we no longer have any overt opponents of European unity," though there were some within who "make use of counterfeit problems as one would use counterfeit money—to deceive people"; and he then set about to deny such supposedly *faux problèmes*.

The "perspective has also been complicated by the use of the analogy with a single, federal state which has been characteristic of 'Europeans' within and outside the Six"; again partly as a "deliberate blurring of the line between today's reality and tomorrow's hope," writes Mrs. Camps. And in the view of Dr. Alting von Geusau (writing in *Internationale Spectator*), apart from these tactics, discussion has been made elusive by the way many Europeans "stick to the original concepts in spite of fundamental changes in European and international relations." The group set up some years ago by the Council of Europe to look into the problem of European unity conceded in its sober re-appraisal, *Europe and the Europeans,* that "no clear picture emerged from this intimate and searching discussion," only "the need for genuine realism"; but M. Denis de Rougemont, though he acted as chairman of the group, stuck to "federation" in an introduction didactic and waspish in tone, which read as if he neither heard what the group said nor read the thoughtful summary which followed.

The study also admitted that the discussion left only a sense of the paucity of political inventiveness. One need therefore be neither for nor against the idea of European union to find exciting interest in any concrete instance of the anxious quest for some political idea that might work effectively beyond the nation-state and before the unlikely prospect of something like a world state. But for the reasons mentioned earlier, the student still has to sort out some of the quite non-partisan issues that crop up continually, such as what is "political" and what is not, by working back to general findings of political science and even to traditional tenets of political theory. The scope of this paper is precisely such an attempt, inevitably a modest one, to clarify some of the political elements of European union. Only a relatively small part of the vast literature has concerned itself with the political side, and the bulk of this with the "diplomatic" aspects, such as the position of Great Britain and the crosscurrent of Atlantic Union.[1] Here we are concerned rather with the "constitutional" side, and not much

[1] Apart from the more historical study by Ernst Haas, *The Unity of Europe, 1950–57* (London, 1958), and the same writer's theoretical "International Integration: The European and the Universal Process," *International Organization* (Boston), Summer 1961, perhaps the most helpful are the two most recent—the informed and careful study by Miriam Camps, *What Kind of Europe?* (London, 1965), and the special issue of *Internationale Spectator* (The Hague), April 8, 1965, with twenty essays by well-known Dutch experts and scholars. A more international group contributed some useful papers to the Conference of the Grotius Seminarium on "Limits and Problems of European Integration" (ed. B. Landheer, The Hague, 1963).

with actual structure and organization, amply described and discussed elsewhere, but as a general system in itself and in relation to a wider international system.

A New Political System?

It would be natural to start from what exists, but on the political side one cannot do even that without some clarification, as there are many divergences of mind among leading "Europeans." Most of them had from the outset called for federation. When initiating the first working institution, the European Coal and Steel Community—though its Charter said nothing of the sort—M. Robert Schuman insisted that it was but the first rung of the federal ladder; but later in the group set up by the Council of Europe both he and Mr. van Kleffens spoke of nothing more precise than integration. Nor did the Treaty of Rome include any political premise in its substantive part, but its preamble clearly if indefinitely stated the intention of the signatories to work for "a closer political union." The governments have made some acknowledgment in the abortive Fouchet-Cattani proposals, and the "European" views have been given more precise and authoritative expression in the several reports prepared for the European parliament by its political committee. But Dr. Hallstein dismissed in his lecture the whole "distinction between economic and political unification as specious. . . . What is called economic fusion is in fact a political process." To add to it defense and foreign policy "would not represent a transition to another, the 'political' sphere but would be merely the addition of further matters in a process which in fact already belongs to the political sphere." The division of views came out sharply in two speeches earlier in the year. On January 9, 1964, Dr. Erhard insisted in the Bundestag that "Europe cannot be achieved by automatic progress within the framework of the Rome Treaties, i.e., solely in the field of economic integration. . . .

It will take all our endeavours and all our political will to gather
Europe into a unit that is not just technocratic but also political."
On his side, in his speech to the European parliament on June 18,
Dr. Hallstein went so far as to list a "specious political union" as
one of the dangers facing the Community.

Whatever may lie behind Dr. Hallstein's line of argument, it
enters deeply into the actual nature of the new European arrangements; and to find their place in the range of current political
experiments it may help, before discussing specific modes, to see in
a general way what political union really implies. Dr. Hallstein's
argument no doubt is correct in this sense and degree: The Six
being a group of independent states, any decision to do something
in common, from a solitary act to the EEC, can be taken only by
the governments; and in all such cases the *agents* and the *instruments* are both political. But the *object* can be non-political (a
commercial treaty or the ECSC), and the agency charged with the
execution, even if autonomous, like the ECSC, would be essentially an administrative organ. As Dr. Erhard put it in his speech,
in the Common Market powers have been given "not to what
might be termed in any democratic sense a politically responsible
body, but only to a joint administration." Such an organ is competent to manage the activity put in its charge, within the terms of
the agreement, but not to act in any other sectors of economic and
social life of the members, let alone in any political matter.

Perhaps a point open to argument is how far such non-political
activities can range without guidance and control from a political
organ. Dr. Hallstein again diverges from the predominant European view when he insists that the EEC does not need it; he points
out that the Treaty of Rome did not lay down a margin beyond
which "it can be implemented only on condition that 'political
union' has been achieved." In this he seems to be supported by
Professor Kymmel, who notes (in *Internationale Spectator*) that
Benelux is in effect a common market but without any political

superstructure. "In my view a common market or economic integration can be established and maintained without federation and without centralizing all elements of economic policy in a supernational or federal body"—though Dr. Hallstein, one presumes, would like to see all those elements centralized at Brussels, which happens to make all the difference.

To come back to the main argument, this particular difference of view affects only the range of non-political activities, but the position is very different where the object is also political—e.g., a diplomatic or a military alliance. Even if limited in scope and time (and though, like NATO, it may boast a supreme commander), it could never be wholly autonomous. The task itself can never be defined and limited in advance but must remain a continuous variable reflecting changing situations, and situations changed by the conduct of the opposing parties as much as by the intent of the united parties, and so calling for equally continuous adaptations in policy. Every decision, possibly charged with issues of peace or war, must inevitably stay with the responsible governments. But if they should reach the point where they want to unify and make permanent both the process of decision-making and that of execution in what by its nature must remain a variable political sphere, foreign policy and defense, that could only mean a common executive authority: that is—whatever its form and the process of gestation—a common government. Within possible constitutional variations, that is the essence of political union.

The six partners in the EEC, as Professor Kymmel points out, have never stated unambiguously how they saw the end product of "closer political integration." All the student has to go by are the Fouchet-Cattani proposals and the *desiderata* of the political committee of the European parliament as offering such formal evidence as there is; and all one can do is to see how these relate to accepted patterns of political theory and experience. But even that is only half the problem. There are two sides to any political picture—its form and its fitness. Form is the visible and classifiable element, but what makes it right or wrong is the second component of any political system, the social ambience in which it has to operate. If the governments, which must carry the consequences of their words, have shrunk from being more precise on what they had in mind, the "Europeans" through years of insistent pressure have failed to probe into the utterly new social climate for which with unquestioning assurance they have offered an old transatlantic plant. As Mr. Thornton Read remarked recently, with a touch of impatient sharpness, "In politics as in war certainty is a symptom of blindness."

The Regional Fallacy

The restlessness which now makes life uneasy all the world over springs from a combination of two revolutionary currents: (1) the end of the colonial era and the mass-making of new states, and (2) at the same time, a universal social revolution which through economic planning for social security and welfare is hardening every state into something more truly organic than anything known before; and all that has to be fitted into the high effort to build up a lasting international system of law and order. This is the world we face now. To pass the test of historic fitness any political experiment will have to take in the first two verities, which seem irreversible, and help to contain and guide them toward the third, so that we may complete the democratic ladder of responsible government. Perhaps in 1919 this ideal was premature; nuclear power and the opening up of space have now made it the foremost priority within which every other human aspiration—communal and individual, material and moral—is inescapably enmeshed. The reaction to the Second World War brought up pleas for world government and world federation, while others retreated into ideas for regional union as an intermediate stage between the national state and the world. It all depends whether it is meant to promote closed and exclusive regional unions or simply for administrative devolution within a universal system. "Given the complexities of modern life and the restlessness of the mass of new states, it is evident that the demands likely to be made upon any central international authority are bound to be very heavy, and perhaps excessive," the present writer suggested to the Grotius Seminarium. "It might be all to the good if that burden could be relieved by entrusting regional groups with the right and duty to deal in the first instance with any local issues through regional councils and regional courts, with the right of appeal to the central council and court should the local effort fail. . . . Such a scheme of devolution would also have politically an educational value in that it would encourage the local groups . . . through the exercise of direct responsibility to learn the need for, and the habit of, give-and-take in their mutual relations" —as proximity and likeness have not always bred political tolerance among them. It might also, as a secondary advantage, help to ease the problem of representation at the center.

The possible use of such regional devolution has hardly been explored so far. But the regional idea would have vastly different consequences if used to set up closed political units. "The new units would then not support but would cut across the jurisdiction and authority of any international system. The argument about the need of an intermediate step is obviously only valid if the regional unions are to be open unions; whereas if they are to be closed and exclusive unions, the more fully and effectively they are integrated the deeper must in fact be the division they cause in the emergent unity of the world." Most of its "European" champions have seen their regional union as leading, from the start or by speedy stages, to a federal state; and experienced men like Schuman, Spaak, Monnet, and others have urged a Western union also as an essential base for any global unification. So had Mazzini and his friends been devoutly convinced that the nation-state was the essential

gateway to a world at peace. But it is curious, and perhaps sugges-
tive, that the idea should find favor now when it no longer makes
sense politically or economically, and certainly not historically. It
did not present itself at all to the mind of the two Hague conferences at the turn of the century, and the Covenant of 1919 touched
it but cautiously. A regional emendation was suggested in 1923
but was quickly rejected. It was tried in the Locarno treaties of
1926 but achieved even locally no more than a momentary easing
of strain. Miss Sarah Wambaugh, the American jurist, pointed out
some years ago that after the First World War, Europe and Asia
on the one side and the U.S. on the other tried two opposite
approaches to security based on differing philosophies. The League
system could not be tried out fully as long as America remained
neutral; the American system had a free run, but insofar as they
were regional systems neither worked. "The League system did not
fail because it was not regional, but rather because it was regional
in effect." "Geographical association no longer corresponds to the
actual interests of neighbors"—a view echoed later in the group
appointed by the Council of Europe, that the interests of Western
countries now overflow in all directions. She quoted from Carl
Hambro that "it is the sea and air lanes, not overland continental
traffic, that hold us together in close association."

From an international standpoint this is merely quoting the
obvious. But even from a regional position it seems strange that it
should spring into favor in Western Europe. The early European
dreamers of world peace—Crucé and St. Pierre, Kant and Rous-
seau, and the rest—never thought of it; to them Europe was their
universe. In later days of trade and colonial expansion Europe
wanted to be the universe, and the Concert of Europe was the
controlling voice of the political world. Is there some meaning in
the fact that this urge for European union should have come when
Europe no longer dominates? Europe created "nationality," but
out of the same fount of liberating principles it also created inter-

nationalism. Yet now, when its ideas have spread to the four quarters of the globe and the prospect seems ripe at last for a general system, Europe is being urged to shrink back within the narrow comforts of her own walls. Western union—like Great Britain's eventual connection with it—has been urged above all as essential for economic well-being through the creation of a large-scale common market. A paper from the Council of Europe had summarized the economic case in the simple proposition that national markets were too small, while world integration was impracticable.[2] The argument thus relies (1) on an outdated physical-political antithesis; and from that it proceeds to (2) the "specious" assumption that national markets were the normal economic working unit, ignoring the immense web of international trade and also the numerous intra-national links in all the main sectors of production.

It seems a doubtful issue, but I am neither competent to discuss it nor concerned with economic regionalism except in its political repercussions.[3] And as to these, whatever the material results, the

[2] Research Directorate of the Secretariat-General of the Council of Europe, *The Present State of Economic Integration in Western Europe* (Strasbourg, July 1955), p. 94.

[3] As references to the economic success of the United States are especially persistent, one may refer to the paper by S. Dell, "Economic Integration and the American Example," in *The Economic Journal,* March 1959. (1) It quotes the studies of the late L. Rostas to the effect that "relative productivity is in no way related to the size of the market. This points to the fact that the optimum plant (or firm) and specialization can be achieved within the limits of a smaller market" (e.g., Swedish and Swiss metallurgical achievement). (2) It quotes as "particularly damaging" the findings of Erwin Rothbarth and others that United States industry was more efficient than British industry as long ago as 1870, if not earlier, when its internal market was smaller than the English market. (3) It doubts whether regional per capita income differences are now any smaller in the United States, with its vast integrated economy, than in Western Europe, with its patchwork of independent states. It thus refutes the assumption that economic integration by itself leads to greater productivity and to uniform development throughout a large region.

mercantilist practices of economic planning will of necessity have to be applied still more forcefully in a regional union, which will have so many more strands to readjust and pull together, than in any one state. There must be something in the fact that whereas in England a co-ordinating Ministry of Economic Affairs was set up only in the autumn of 1964 by a new Labour government, the Common Market of six sovereign states was from the outset placed under the management of an essentially bureaucratic commission. The same considerations apply with even greater force to the political factors. In their case the common interest cannot be visibly defined, while they often touch imponderable and fugitive sentiments. To build up a cohesive loyalty national movements have often had to disinter or invent all sorts of historical, social, and emotional affinities, above all to keep alive the fear of some common external danger. Regionalism, starting with more differences than affinities, would have to go even further in that. Western union has been argued all along as vital for putting Europe in a state of economic and political self-defense, "to avoid coming under Russian domination without at the same time accepting permanent American overlordship," though some supporters might wish to reverse the order of precedence of the two nightmares. Western man used to pride himself on his humanistic cosmopolitan outlook, but now even men of standing have come to talk of the need to develop a "European personality." It would not be fair to saddle them with the aberrations of Count Coudenhove-Kalergi, the first recipient of the Charlemagne prize, who in his *Pan-Europa* and other writings has discovered a "Western nationality," a "European race," and even a "European soul" emphatically different from the American soul; but what is that European personality? Does it begin and end at the limits of the Common Market? Even the formal Martino Report to the European parliament can say that "there is no question of dissolving Europe in a wider ensemble in which her personality would be lost"! In the nature of things it must be something that both binds and divides, and by implication also something which is not there but has to be brought into being. Indeed, one general reason for demanding an elected parliament seems to be a belief that "direct elections are the best, perhaps the only way of stimulating mass interest and participation in European unification."

The making of "Europe" is not to be kept merely to economics and politics, but has to bring into relief also *"l'unité du patrimoine spirituel et culturel de l'Europe,"* says the Martino Report. A strange argument in a serious source, in view of the long, sad history of Europe's political and religious divisions, many more and fiercer than the conflicts with Asia and the Americas, and now again cut in half ideologically. As I have said in the Grotius volume, if there is a "unique characteristic of European civilization, in contrast with Eastern and other civilizations, it is that it always has been an *open* civilization . . . [and so] able to permeate the whole world with her political, social, and cultural outlook and experience. . . ."[4] When one thinks of the past humanistic glories of the ancient universities of Paris and Oxford, of Prague and Bologna, how strange it is to be faced now, just when science is opening up the farthest ways to outer space and the planets"—and when with our Ariel-like means of communication all knowledge is instantly "universalized"—to be faced with a proposal for a "European University where things are to be taught from a specifically 'European' angle, so as to reinforce Europe's cultural and scientific potential." Perhaps it is not odd but in character that this narrowing scheme should have been put into the Euratom Treaty— although the new university is to teach also economics and politics, sociology and psychology!

[4] Europe has had "an unusually dynamic history"; "the end of the European Age in history is not necessarily the end of Europe, or of a civilization which, though inseparable from the European heritage, has ceased to be exclusively European." Oscar Halecki, *The Limits and Divisions of European History* (London, 1950), p. 21.

Will the new "third world," which is so eager for knowledge and development, and in which we have to compete with new revolutionary influences, not suspect any cultural product labeled as distinctly European? The very concept of a closed regional union is a contradiction of the historic European idea; and the farther it moves from the sheer material sector, the more does its synthetic nature stand exposed. But even if these inbreeding efforts and devices—closed economic planning, exclusive political institutions, the cultivation of a regional patriotism—even if all this were to serve the goal of a (limited) European union, it can hardly bear the argument that it also is the highway to a wider international unity.

"Whatever proclaims a difference creates a division," said Dr. Johnson. The ecumenical argument for European union has carried least conviction of all, and not only among outsiders. One may quote a few points of doubt from within the movement, not because they are critical but because they are evident and restore the balance of view. As to inwardness, it seems likely to Dr. J. L. Heldring that in its first period it would be "so concentrated on the task of keeping a precarious union together and creating an identity of its own that it would have little time and energy left for acquiring a global vision and tackling global tasks. It would not be the first time in history when a new nation would seek strength in isolation." Dr. Hallstein in fact sees this to be inevitable: "There is no public association, no State and no association of States which does not begin by attending to the welfare and security of its own members. [This is] the *raison d'être* of every political community." As to outlook, in the view of Dr. Von Geusau "the very penetration into these fields [foreign policy and defense] tends to divert attention among the Six from the aim of being a stepping-stone for better international co-operation, to that of merely becoming a new 'big power' "—Dr. Hallstein's "sovereign voice." "There is no special reason to believe that a federal Europe would suddenly be guided exclusively by sweet reasonableness and self-restraint," says Dr. Heldring. And a leading Dutch parliamentarian, Mr. G. M. Nederhorst, has warned that "in the perspective of the next ten or twenty years the idea of Europe as a 'third force' will look even more unrealistic than it does today." As to the limits of the union, he went on, the search for a true European solution "requires more than a solution of little Europe within the framework of the six, the seven, or the fifteen. The task which the European federalists set themselves in the resistance movement during the first post-war years to create in Europe the political and social conditions for an all-European peace still remains to be solved. This is a program which does not accept as inevitable the *status quo* thrust upon us by Soviet policy."[5]

The Federal Fallacy

Of the many assumptions which have gone into the making of the "European" creed the most persistent has been the idea of federation; and the federal idea in fact traverses most aspects and issues of European union, both in its internal organization and in its relation to the wider international problem. It is an old idea which has appeared often in plans and literature, but all that has little to say on the substance of the present appeal, except that it always expressed some antagonism. The republican call in the middle of the nineteenth century, with Victor Hugo in the lead, for a European union of "free peoples" was little beyond a radical holy alliance in the struggle against autocracy; and Cobden's shrill call

[5] Even M. Jean Monnet, who among "Europeans" stands on a distinguished level of his own, could claim through the recent declaration of his Action Committee that European union was the best way to achieve German reunification. Does it not seem obvious instead, as Russia refuses to recognize the EEC, fears the consolidation of a Western political union in which she believes Germany would be dominant, that she would be less likely to give up her hold on the buffer formed by Eastern Germany?

in 1856 was pointedly aimed at Russia. The Pan-Europa vicariously urged after the First World War was both anti-Bolshevik and anti-Anglo-Saxon, but it never had any solid outline or more than a dubious and changeable support.

Of the inter-war schemes, that proposed by Briand in 1929 was the only solid one, and also the only one to offer some comparison with the present ideas. Though it came before the nuclear explosion and the mass of new states, the overwhelming view was that any European union must avoid all exclusiveness and must remain an organic part of the League of Nations; and at Geneva most governments feared that, "no matter what the intentions of its promoters, the Continental union might drain the League of Nations of its substance and compromise its universality"—therefore they favored economic but not political action. The idea of European union could hardly have been a natural product as it never led to actual unity. The present call for a federal union is something quite new; it goes further in scope, but as a consequence it also is narrower in outlook. As its advocates hope to make Europe free of the new American power by emulating its successful federal formula, a brief look at the American analogy should throw light on the fitness of the idea for international integration under the conditions of our time.

When, in spite of the crisis, the Supreme Court threw out the National Recovery Act in 1935, President Roosevelt pointed out that in the "horse-and-buggy" days when the Constitution was written, some 90 per cent of the population lived in self-sufficient local communities. Even more to the point, the view of democracy then ruling wanted government to do as little as possible, and the federal system was shaped to that outlook. It was an invention meant to deal with a revolutionary situation and to unite thirteen undeveloped states on an isolated continent, and with "more common problems coming to them in the future than they had separate history binding them to the past." The revolutionary situation of the nuclear age hardly answers to a pattern which gave every citizen an absolute right to carry arms. To be at all valid the analogy would have, in the first place, to reflect not what happened nearly 200 years ago, but whether, if the forty-eight states had each developed to full separate political and economic independence, they could be induced to federate now. Concrete evidence for an answer is supplied by the difficulties which all the old federal governments have met since the war in the everyday performance of their tasks—in such non-political matters as highways and banking and health services, etc.—in Canada and Australia as in America; even in placid Switzerland most of the referenda since the war have gone against the federal government. They have even been faced with threats of secession from Quebec and Western Australia, and in the U.S. after 200 years and a bloody civil war, the issue of states' rights still remains a perennial irritant.

Sometimes these federal governments have actually been helped by international commitments in matters in which they were obstructed by their own internal constitutions. All that can still happen in federations which by now are well-established national societies. Yet the reaction is not unnatural. A federal system rests upon a settled balance of power; any addition to the central functions alters that balance and with cumulative and permanent effect. But wider evidence shows that it is not merely a matter of holding on to the letter of an old compact, but more generally a reaction to the new tendencies of government. We have not sufficiently noted the centrifugal internal regionalism which in recent years has arisen or hardened also in old unitary states—in Belgium as in Italy, in France, and in Great Britain and, significantly, in the new federation of India. India had been provided with a more modern constitution and had inherited a unified administration and a strong sense of national unity forged in the struggle for independence; yet since then she has been troubled by cross-regional strains which had not existed before and has had to accept new anachronistic sub-divisions in the shape of language and such states. This widespread experience must mean that one effect of centralized planning is to repel local sections with marked interests or characteristics of their own, and that the reaction inevitably turns the mind to disunion. It should be obvious that the wider the limits of association and the more disparate the parts, the more difficult it must prove to accommodate the marginal elements.[6]

The "European" federalists have been so fascinated by a readily convenient formula that they have neither asked how it works where it exists, nor whether its origins bear any relation to the problem of uniting a group of states in the present social ambience. It is this question of sociological fitness which is at issue here. But once again one has first to interpolate a theoretical clarification, because the tactical vagueness of the "Europeans" has now been fed by a new thesis from Professor Carl Friedrich, who has a close knowledge of the European experiment and is a reputed authority on the federal idea. In two papers (for an Oxford meeting on federation, in September 1963, and at the Sixth World Congress of I.P.S.A., Geneva, September 1964) Professor Friedrich has tried to replace the established meaning of federation as a particular type of political union with the idea of a "process by which a number of

---

[6] It should also be obvious that the "federalizing process" (see below) will remain very brittle until fully accomplished. In the interim period nothing is agreed beyond an intention, as in the Rome treaty, and any change of government in the participating states may bring changes of outlook and intention. "Experience shows that political trends often change in certain countries with disconcerting swiftness" and sharply alter policy, "merely as a consequence of the normal working of democratic institutions and not because of any calculated Machiavellism" (Jan Hostie, in *Regionalism and World Organization,* 1944). Political attempts must remain exposed to politics. The late Dr. Hugh Dalton, e.g., insisted that British Labour could join in a European union only with other socialist governments. Therefore, says Mr. Hostie, "international institutions must be built to withstand at least the likeliest of the political shifts"— which seems possible only through functional arrangements.

separate political organizations, be they states or any other kind of association, enter into arrangements" for doing various things jointly. Any and all of these actions belong into a general "federalizing process." Even in old federations, he says, there is never a constant position between unifying and diversifying forces; rather an oscillating process with sometimes one, sometimes the other in the ascendant. That is no doubt true, but it is true of all government; and it is least true of federal government. A new union or association is not conceivable without some formal compact, whose main purpose is precisely to delimit the competence of the various organs. That is why it has to provide for an arbitral court, which Professor Friedrich lists among the essentials of a federal framework, and why it generally puts stiff obstacles in the way of that process of change—which Professor Friedrich thinks should be not as difficult as it is in the U.S., but neither "so easy that the federation will not hold together." The very purpose of any such written compact or statute is precisely to introduce the factor of fixity in the index of power; and nothing is so fixed as a federal constitution. It is intended to withstand the constant pressures from the ordinary claims of government as from sectional interests, and so "hold together" the whole. It has been far easier to change the position and powers of the British Crown by what one may fairly call a functional adaptation, than it has been to change the position and powers of the federal authority in the U.S. or Canada or Australia by amendment of their written constitutions.

"The function of a true political thinker," said the late Professor Hobhouse, "is not to predict events, but to point out causal connections." With all political systems now shaken by a social revolution, it is all the more the part of the political scientist to try to project the true implications of the schemes and expedients of the practicing politician; whereas the likely effect of such permissive teaching is illustrated by Dr. Hallstein's lecture—to use an experienced and authoritative case. He starts from a correct statement of established theory: "The position is that federation is one state but the confederation is a league of states." After that his thought becomes elusive. The Community would leave to "each member its ultimate sovereign power," but it had to be a "firm union" and it must speak with "a 'sovereign' voice in world politics." To that end, after economic and social life, trade and foreign policy and "the sinews of war must be made Community matter," leading to the "integration of defense policy." "Integration is thus a process and not a static thing, and this process is one that tends toward complete federation, that is to a federal state." And the argument ends in the dismantling of the initial statement: "The conclusion is that there is no hard distinction between federation and confederation, obliging us to choose."[7]

We have not been helped by such recent inflationary usage of "democracy"; yet that is an abstract generic term which might be filled with any content, from *laissez faire* to socialist planning. But terms of specific constitutional classification are meant to tell us within fairly clear limits what kind of political prospect we are called upon to underwrite with our votes. That is all the more proper in a new and far-reaching political adventure, and for an electorate which so far has nowhere been faced yet by a special

---

[7] Professor Friedrich's "any kind of association" presumably could mean that OEEC and COMECON, EFTA and NATO and the Arab League are all engaged in a "federalizing process," whether they mean it or not. The kind of confusing guidance which such terminological license can bring was offered to the Oxford conference by Professor W. H. Morris-Jones, as quoted by Professor Friedrich (Geneva paper, note 10): "The Commonwealth, although as a whole it is no kind of federalism, can usefully be regarded as a collection of partial, functional, intermittent federations, composed of different members at different times for different purposes." No other authorities have suggested such an inflation of the federal idea. One need not go back to the classical work of Jellinek, but among leading contemporary writers neither Professor C. K. Wheare, in general theory, nor Professor A. L. Goodhardt, as an authority on the American system, has propounded anything of the kind.

"European" party or by a special election on a clear issue of European union. Could an election for a European parliament ask the electorate from Bremen to Brindisi simply to "vote for our federalizing process"? The thesis is all the more dubious from such a learned source because at the same time Professor Friedrich prescribes (with one exception) all the orthodox ingredients as necessary for a federal framework: an arbitral court and provision for amendments—both of which imply not only a written but a firm constitution—and a joint working executive; and if a federal executive no doubt also a federal parliament. And here we come to those matters which are at the heart of the European problem, as of any political system, namely, the range of its functions and the conditions under which they have to be performed. Fortunately there is one aspect on which all students of politics are likely to be agreed—the vast change in the nature of government and, as a consequence, in the respective positions of executive and parliament. The original intent of the democratic idea was "that Government should be kept to a minimum, and that minimum was to be guided by an informed and sensible electorate and controlled by its independent representatives." In all these respects we have gone far toward the opposite pole, even in democratic countries, as I ventured to say a few years ago. "Government now tends to be omnipresent and, where present, almost omnipotent, if we accept, as we must, Sir Ernest Barker's definition that government authority is 'the sum of its functions.' " For any new federal experiment, if meant to be free to develop the modern attributes of a welfare society, the working prototype is likely to be not the U.S. Constitution of 1787 but something nearer to the federal system of the U.S.S.R.

The two functions always conceded as belonging to a federal executive have been defense and foreign policy (and trade). Defense as recently as 1914 was still a matter of a limited force with a limited armory; but which part of resources and of industrial potential could now be said to remain outside the range of Dr. Hallstein's "sinews of war"—and not only in time of war but throughout the longer periods of peace? Which part of economic and financial policy is now outside the scope of foreign policy? Nor is it possible to envisage any limit to the spread of centralized public action; the continuous pressure for new inventions and discoveries, on which the economic sector is as dependent as defense, can generally be controlled and provided for only by some central authority. The political balance sheet of these considerations should be self-evident. If the all-inclusive union which the "Europeans" want were to be based on a restrictive federal balance of power it would not be capable of growing freely into the kind of planned welfare society which marks our time; whereas if it were to be set up without the traditional federal restraints, it must grow—as it would have more, and more mixed, elements to weld together—into a more unitary political system than any existing federation.[8]

"The sum of these functions," not any preconceived formula, must in the end shape the character of an eventual European executive, and hence also of a European parliament. As executive and parliament will be the pivotal organs of any fully fledged union—we may ignore for this brief review the piquant question of

[8] Dr. J. W. Beijen, Dutch financial expert and diplomat, has recently insisted on the importance of the social task, saying that a modern government could not give up its freedom to use economic and financial policy for social ends unless that responsibility were taken over by some common authority. "The European Communities were conceived to do just that. . . . Too often the Communities are still considered as merely a means to increase the economic strength of the area. In essence, their task in the social field is fundamental." The inclusion of agriculture enhances that aspect, for everywhere agricultural policy is "foremost social policy and only secondary economic policy. It is the conduct of social policy which makes the Community into something different in essence from other forms of economic co-operation between governments." *Internationale Spectator,* pp. 466–67.

who would be its head, an elected president with hereditary kings and queens under him, or perhaps the several national rulers by rotation—it is striking how perfunctorily they have been treated in the prolific literature on European union; indeed, the nature of the executive has been given hardly a glance. Most of the recent argument has expressed an anxiety to give the European parliament some real power of control over policy as against that which now falls to the Council of Ministers—the popular as against the governmental factor. The argument has been put with cogency and urgency in the Martino Report and may be justified in itself—as long as the present arrangements last. But it is dubious as a general argument, and peculiar in its immediate assumptions. It is peculiar that a body of delegated parliamentarians should think it possible to be transformed, and fairly speedily, into a representative parliament, with commensurate powers, without making it clear that this could not be until an equally representative common executive had taken charge of affairs—of affairs intended to spread quickly and widely into new fields. The making of a comprehensive union could hardly be left to an amorphous popular assembly and a commission of "technocrats." And in a more general way, the expectation of commanding powers for such a parliament overlooks the strong contrary current, and one bound to prevail if the wish for full union is fulfilled. One could almost lay it down as a law of modern politics that the powers of executive and parliament are bound to move in inverse ratio to each other. There are three general reasons for this: First, the enormous increase in government activity reduces the possiblity of parliamentary initiative and control; that is bound to be more acute in a multi-state union with its wider jurisdiction and therefore greater complexity in policy-making. Second, the same conditions have added weight to party organization and constricted the independence of individual members (both admitted and justified by the late Lord Morrison in his book *Government and Parliament*). As one cannot foresee how party alignments and organization would develop in an elected European parliament, that is one particular point that must remain open.

The third reason is the most active and relevant. The "wider the activity of the state the wider its direct contacts and relations with organized groups of interest, a trend as conspicuous in Scandinavia as in the U.S. Many points of economic and social policy are now settled, or modified in application, through private bargaining between government departments and professional and other organized groups, without benefit of Parliament."[9] A whole new system of policy-making has thus grown up, not through any arbitrary imposition but through the inescapable sweep and urgencies of planned government, a system of government by committee. This particular tendency, above all others, would inevitably be strongly at work in a new multi-state union. Its administration could hardly work unless it were preponderantly bureaucratic. The wider and more varied the jurisdiction to be encompassed, the firmer will its planning have to be, and in the same measure less amenable to protracted debate and detailed control by a motley parliamentary chamber at the center. Local variations in claims and interests, and the multiplicity of organized groups, could not be attended to in any other way so as to gain acceptance for uniform legislation and administrative rules. While, therefore, it is a fair claim that the present communities (though it was not true of ECSC) fall short in democratic content as long as they lack a representative assembly, it is an illusion to think that in a "more perfect union" an elected parliament will gather unto itself more power than is now left to national parliaments even in the best of democratic states. It is likely to be less. It will have neither the cohesion nor the acquired traditions of a national parliament, while the executive will

[9] David Mitrany, *Parliamentary Affairs,* Winter 1955–56, p. 19. A few years ago an American observer of the British administrative scene, Professor Samuel Beer of Harvard, went so far as to describe what he had seen as "quasi-corporatism."

be under greater pressure of public business but also less exposed to the watchfulness of parties and press and popular opinion. Warning that "Europe is not a nation," the secretary-general of the European parliament, Dr. H. R. Nord, went on to say that "it follows that attempts should not be made to solve the problem of European parliamentary control merely by trying to make the European Parliament look more like a national one. We are faced with a new and original phenomenon and the future role of the Parliament should be assessed in the light of the distribution of power within the Community."

Because of the neglect of such an assessment some other derivative aspects of the parliamentary problem have been passed by altogether. The European parliament has for some years pressed for direct elections with universal suffrage so as "to associate the peoples" in the work of political integration, though as members of their home parliaments they must be aware of the spreading apathy of mass electorates everywhere. Constituencies are too large for close contact and persuasion, and the public issues too many and too technical to allow for more than very broad party appeals at election time. What range of constituencies could serve for an oversize continental election—a million, two million names on the electoral roll? What kind of concrete "European" issues could be put by candidates to so vast and mixed an electorate to make as good sense in Sicily as in Brabant, on the Ruhr and in Brittany, so as to produce that common "European consciousness"? That brings up a final and a more serious issue than the awkwardness of electoral mechanics. A fair European consciousness has been achieved at Strasbourg by the simple device of keeping the anti-Europeans out. It was perhaps not unnatural to send to Strasbourg party members who at least were in general sympathy with the institution. But it was a drastic act to exclude the Communists altogether when they are such a formidable electoral force in Italy and in France. What is to be done about this in a general election? Only two alternatives seem possible: (1) submit to the fundamentals of universal suffrage and so let in from the start a powerful element opposed to the very idea of Western union and allied ideologically to the hostile communist world; or (2) exclude the Communists and so pollute the democratic claim from the start. This, moreover, may make them the gathering core for other dissident elements and so, paradoxically, on this issue help to widen their national appeal and make their outcast status still more indefensible.

Perhaps there is no more curious sidelight into the state of mind, or the tactics, of the "Europeans" than the way they have all along assumed that direct elections by universal suffrage must bring them popular support. The probability has simply been ignored that such a direct electoral challenge would also provide the first occasion when the various, now still disjointed, groups and sections who for one reason or another dislike or doubt the idea of Western union would be brought together into something like an organized opposition.

The Functional Alternative

So much of what precedes had to be given over to a critical examination of the federal idea because what matters here is not its theoretical virtues but its fitness for multi-national association— even within the arbitrary limits of a region. That people should have turned to it is not unnatural; it seemed the only available formula, because our political thinking has been so long rooted in the notion that every authority must be linked to a given territory.[10] For the rest, it is plain that European federalism has been

[10] This came out patly in the criticism of M. J. Petot, that the experience of the European communities shows the unreality of the "functionalist" thesis that starting from small, autonomous specialized authorities one could build a complete state! A complete state and its introverted nature happens to be the very idea which functionalism seeks to overcome internationally. "Des Communautés Européennes à la Fédération," in *Revue Générale de Droit International Public* (Paris, 1960), Vol. 64 (2).

a blend of myth and some very mixed sentiments. That is proved in another way by the readiness of moderate "Europeans" for something more flexible. "The majority of us do not regard the unification of Europe with the emotions of people acquiring a new fatherland," writes Professor Samkalden (in *Internationale Spectator*); there is a need for "a diversity of new organizations for specific needs and interests," and a plurality of them is already available in which the value of the European communities, "but also their necessary limitation, find clear expression."

New and original phenomena demand, as at other crossroads in history, suitable changes in the government of societies, and three such phenomena may be singled out as governing the present problem of international peace and development: (1) The new scientific inventions and discoveries have raised political, social, and moral issues which can be dealt with only on their own global scale. Not one of them is peculiar to Europe; in the nuclear field all that Western Europe can do is add its own pile of nuclear bombs, but not halt their fearful menace. (2) At the same time we face the contrary prospect of twice the number of independent states entitled by their sovereign status to follow their own will, and many tempted by a revolutionary mood to do so. (3) The third factor, cutting across the other two and confusing their relation, is the trend to neo-mercantilist planning. It has injected the political element into well-nigh all the manifold international activities and relations which formerly grew freely across most frontiers. That is the given equation. The key we have to find is how in these conditions "to harmonize the actions" economic and social, in the words of the U.N. Charter, "in the attainment of common ends." To have lasting effect the solution must be global. In theory it could be done through a world state or federation, but even if desirable such a monstrous construction could hardly come about except through conquest. Or it can be done by making use of the present social and scientific opportunities to link together particular activities and interests, one at a time, according to need and acceptability, giving each a joint authority and policy limited to that activity alone. That is the functional way.

Let it be said at once that there is nothing new in that. It was the natural mode of Western international relations, some public and many private, before the two world wars, but since then we have moved backward from the liberal nineteenth century. "Before 1914 world integration was proceeding steadily by means of firm treaties and relationships, open-door arrangements and so on," wrote Mr. Adolf Drucker. "In addition, a great number of pre-1914 agreements created what might be termed 'abstract regions' through multi-lateral contracts under the authority of international law."[11] Now, as in former autocratic times, economic, social, and even cultural relations have fallen under the control of the state; "the State has almost become an organization for the prevention of free international intercourse and the growth of a normal human society." Fichte's eighteenth-century academic aberration, *Der Geschlossene Handelstaat,* is looming before us as a twentieth-century contingent reality. The trend is general, varying only in manner and degree, and informed with a ruthless pragmatism which permits any government in the name of its "plan" to change policy and practice abruptly without regard to the effect on the interests and plans of other peoples and the hurt to international good will. As their problems are more acute and their ways less staid, the new undeveloped states are especially apt to resort to such planned license; and as at the same time they are now protected by the incipient collective system of the U.N., they can indulge—as no Great Power would have dared in the days of so-called international anarchy—in what is also a new phenomenon and can only be described as "total sovereignty."

That is the new world which somehow has to be brought back

---

[11] One should note the erudite work of Professor François Perroux, who uses the conception of *éspaces économiques* freed from "the servitudes of localization." See, e.g., *L'Europe sans Rivages* (Paris, 1954).

into working relationships, to open up a prospect and provide the elements for international government. We do not know what kind of international government will work. But we do know that as government is only a framework which enables a social community to live its life well, international government can have little sense or body without a living international community. One new phenomenon at least opens up a positive and remarkable prospect in that direction. As was said before, the immediate impact of planning, with its spreading concern for social welfare and rights, is nationalistic. But, as I suggested to the Section on Human Rights at the Sixth I.P.S.A. Congress, in 1964, in its "external aspect one central characteristic is that it is *universal*. I believe this to be a novel, a unique historical situation. In the traditional category of human rights there have always been differences from place to place in attitude, concepts, and practice. But now, whatever their constitutional form or cultural tradition, *all* countries have adopted the philosophy and claims of social security; and hence, inevitably, also similar machinery of administrative practice and controls." If this reading be correct, two practical factors are already at work, and on a world scale, to which strands of functional co-operation could be made fast. One is the indispensable factor of a common outlook and purpose, which in this case puts into strong relief an evident identity of everyday social aims and policy. The other is the useful factor of close similarity of ways and means. Administrative law is implicitly functional law, and so is administrative practice. Every functional link helps to build up a common legal order—as the ILO well exemplifies—specific but also concrete and cumulative, one which does not stay aloof in the atmosphere of diplomatic and juridical pacts but which enters everywhere into the daily life of the peoples themselves.

Two general considerations may be cited in support of this thesis. A general wish for a collective security system was natural after the shock of two world wars and of the atom bomb; but new and remarkable were the first signs of a sense of world community, of international responsibility for local conditions everywhere. The idea of the welfare state, new as it is even in our own countries, is already broadening into a sentiment for a welfare world. The substantial and manifold efforts and contributions generally known as technical assistance are tangible proof of that; not, as in the past, occasional charity in some emergency but a continuous program of aid now accepted almost as a responsibility by the richer countries. On the other side, the new states, politically tangled up in aggressively "uncommitted" groups and leagues, have shown themselves eager to join the U.N.'s special agencies and other such bodies, Professor Benjamin Akzin wrote in *New States and International Organizations,* "because the balance of considerations is in favor of such participation"; and they have come to look upon it "as an international asset and a strengthening of their position in the world."

Considerations such as these show why one can find both opportunity and promise in working arrangements as a way of building up an international community. But it also is a natural, not a contrived idea pressed into an existing political mold. Generally speaking it represents a general turn grown out of the living complexities of twentieth-century society. Both devolution and integration tend to go that way, within states as between states. Socialist theory had contemplated some form of centralized control (state socialism or syndicalism or guild socialism) for economic sectors taken over from capitalist enterprise, but when it came to "nationalization," Labour turned instead to the non-political device of autonomous boards and authorities. That has become the normal way for activities which are altogether new—aviation, atomic energy, and so on. The use made of it in existing federations is of special relevance here. In America, in spite of an old and hard-set regionalism, federal departments (such as Defense and Agriculture, the Federal Reserve Board, etc.) make use in their administration of functional regions (single-purpose areas) which vary freely from service to service and seldom coincide with state lines. And so do the hundred or so executive agencies which have come into being especially since the New Deal—which itself was "not fashioned theoretically out of economic or social creeds" but was the wholly pragmatic response to the "felt necessities" of a pressing situation. The clearest evidence can be found in the great experiment of the TVA.

Because its own task could not be performed unless allowed to cut across the sovereign jurisdiction of seven of the United States, the TVA offers a good prototype for possible inter-state arrangements. For the past century and a half a growing number of international unions and services have worked well without reference to political supervision or protection. More specifically, in North America, and apart from the wartime combined boards with Canada, the U.S. since then has become a party to substantial joint activities with neighboring states—the Alcan Highway (a likely model for an eventual Channel tunnel), the St. Lawrence Seaway, the Rio Grande project with Mexico—all of them without any offense to, or intrusion by, the three federal constitutions.

On the other side, as mentioned before, there are a great many cases where a federal constitution has stood in the way of internal functional developments. The TVA indeed itself provides a complete answer. In the face of a pressing social need for such river control, repeated efforts by several presidents since the beginning of the century went astray, until the calamity of the great depression gave Franklin Roosevelt a chance to push through the bill which created the autonomous authority. It was all done by May 1933, within a few weeks of his taking office; but then the TVA had to fight off some forty legal suits over a period of five years and on a variety of constitutional objections before it was allowed to settle down to its great work. "The TVA really introduced a new dimension into the constitutional structure of the U.S., without any change in the Constitution; but it could do so only because it was a new administrative and not a new political dimension."[12]

This is not the place to restate the political philosophy which informs the functional idea, beyond saying that to prefer it to the constitutional approach is not to be timid, much less to be haphazard.[13] "It rests indeed squarely upon the most characteristic idea of the democratic-liberal philosophy, which leaves the individual free to enter into a variety of relationships—religious, political and professional, social and cultural—each of which may take him in different directions and dimensions and into different groupings, some of them of international range. Each of us is in fact a 'bundle' of functional loyalties; so that to build a world community upon such a conception is merely to extend and consolidate it also between national societies and groups." The argument has grown out of a definite view of the dilemma of our time: that we can neither ignore the deep roots of nationality in the search for material efficiency nor deny the urgent cry for social betterment for the sake of a hollow independence. In the face of this dilemma one

---

[12] David Mitrany, *American Interpretations,* London, 1946, pp. 18-20. As against this one must note that President Roosevelt's only "attempt at direct constitutional revision, to increase the membership of the Supreme Court from nine to fifteen, was bitterly disputed and defeated; though in effect it would have meant much less of a constitutional inroad than the experiment of the TVA and the body of new federal executive agencies." *Ibid.,* p. 22.

[13] Some valid theoretical definitions and observations were given already in Georg Jellinek's classic on federalism, *Die Lehre von den Staatenverbindungen,* 1882. Apart from confederations and federations he paid some attention to "administrative unions," with their own organs and a common purpose, which made them a joint administrative area for that task. Thus the International Postal Treaty of 1874 made all treaty states into one vast postal territory in respect to those services. The oldest such unions were set up to ensure free navigation on international rivers, like the Rhine and especially the Lower Danube. The European Danube Commission had greater powers as it was created for the collective interest of Europe and had thus a general international character; it issued regulations and could impose penalties which the member states were bound to

may look briefly at the relative merits of the functional idea in regard to some of those issues which have been shown to raise difficulties for any comprehensive political union.

In the first place, the functional approach does not offend the sentiment of nationality or the pride of sovereignty. Instead of a fictitious formal equality it offers even to the weakest of countries the assurance of non-domination and of an equality of opportunity in the working benefits of any functional activity in which it participates. And these assurances can be the more readily accepted even by touchy ex-colonial states, as Professor Akzin has shown, because functional arrangements have the patent virtue of technical self-determination. The range of their task can be clearly defined, and this in turn makes plain the powers and resources needed for its performance. Internationally speaking, political self-determination in this way is translated into functional co-determination. Allowing for suitable variations, Mrs. Camps has concluded that even for the Common Market "this pattern is likely to be followed in the future, and to be reinforced by the fusion of the Communities, the governments being willing effectively to shift authority to the Commission only when the limits within which the Commission can act have been fairly strictly defined."

This bears closely on the central difficulty of democratic con-

---

enforce, performing in this respect "acts of international legislation," and within its sphere it also had the character of an international court. Though treaties creating these unions were for limited periods and members had the right to withdraw, in effect the nature of their activity made them perpetual, as no state could, e.g., want the dissolution of postal and telegraph services which served the common interests of civilized communities (pp. 158 ff.). (These nineteenth-century precedents suggest how much political trouble they would have saved themselves, while doing service to the whole world community, if at the end of the First World War the Allied Powers had acted not strategically but functionally and internationalized the Dardanelles and the Suez and Panama canals. Now the first is in effect dominated by Russia, whom they meant to keep out; the second in the not too reliable hands of Egypt; and the last a source of friction between the U.S. and the new temper in Latin America.)

trol. As we have said, even in democratic states control over executive and administration has slipped away from parliament. In England (and elsewhere) we have indeed enacted the paradox that industries and services nationalized into public ownership have been exempted from the public control of Parliament, except for a general debate on their annual reports. In this respect, at any rate, international development would seem to show an advance on national practice. For the discussion of general policy the U.N. has the Economic and Social Council; but the significant innovation is that every one of the specialized agencies, including the ILO, has its own little functional assembly, varying with the work of the agency, which meets periodically to review the work done and to lay down policy and fix a budget for the next period. Moreover, Article 71 of the U.N. Charter has given certain private international bodies, the non-governmental organizations, a formal right to be consulted or an informal right to be heard in their particular sphere of interest, and so has established a sort of functional constituency which can influence the agency's policy, but also brings back to the members of their association an insight into the reasons why that policy should be supported. In that way an effective process of democratic representation can be restored; while the doings at Brussels have practically been taken out of the hands of the national parliaments, both the delegates to these functional assemblies and the non-governmental associations know what it is all about and can judge whether a policy is valid and whether it has been carried out fairly.[14]

Bodies such as these may "diminish the orthodox sovereignty of

[14] These functional assemblies have sometimes been confused by critics with functional representation in general bodies, like the economic parliaments popular for a while after the First World War; but in economic parliaments the several groups were there to fight for sectional interests, as in any ordinary parliament; whereas functional bodies represent one interest and one purpose common to them all, and the debate is about ways and means.

the states," wrote Hans Fried some years ago, "but the power and sovereign rights of the people would increase, because they would have a direct voice through their own delegates in all the agencies handling some of their affairs." "People are bad judges of general considerations," was said already by Machiavelli, "but good judges of detail." Apart from these special bodies, the same trend has developed in recent years through national departments negotiating and acting together for many purposes of a technical or practical nature, directly with their opposite branches in other countries; and very often these contacts continue despite political friction. The extent to which the whole practice of foreign policy and relations has thus been revolutionized, in step with the sweep of technical developments and the extension of public controls within each state, can be seen in the mere fact that while three international conferences met in 1853, and about 100 in 1900, their number had increased to some 2,000 by 1953 and now possibly is nearly twice as high. And it is not merely a matter of numbers. We have traveled far from the glittering parade of princes at the Congress of Vienna to the sober meetings of civil servants, scientists, and technicians who through their work now link together sectors of their national life and sections of their national departments into a vast and growing network of peaceful and beneficial international relations.

The same reasons also help to hem in the present inevitable tendency to bureaucracy, both through the clear definition of the scope and powers of a functional authority and through the watchfulness of people who know the work as well as the "technocrats" and have a direct interest in its good performance. The ECSC was organized and worked well on such a basis; whether mixing the three communities will keep these advantages unimpaired remains to be seen. But having pressed out of sheer political zeal for the fusion of the three, many "Europeans," as the Martino Report admits, are now afraid lest the clear supra-nationality of the ECSC should in the process be diluted to the inter-governmental level of the others. Yet it cannot be otherwise: the wider and vaguer the range of its activity, the less is the likelihood that a technical organization would be given the freedom of supra-national autonomy.

The question of membership provides one final point of comparison. A federal system is bound to be closed and exclusive; a functional system is as naturally open, as changes in membership can be absorbed without doing violence to policy and administration. A federal constitution is a balancing act in regard to a whole range of social and political factors: with any change in membership the whole structure may have to be re-organized and probably to be re-negotiated[15]—rather like the Austro-Hungarian *Ausgleich,* which Viennese wits dubbed *"Monarchie auf Kündigung"* because of the inevitable crisis at each ten-year renewal. In fact, Mrs. Camps brings up this very point; at Brussels, too, "there is too much reliance on crises as a technique for forcing decisions." Professor Friedrich's recent thesis is particularly dubious on this point. He would like federal rules to be so easy as to make it possible for some members to leave or for others to be added without breaking up the whole federation. From a wide international experience, on the other hand, Dr. Beijen gives the clear warning that if one really wants to extend the membership of the Common Market "it is better not to speak of federation." Even with the EEC, far as it is from federation, the clause that leaves

---

[15] That this may happen even in old federations was shown at the Canadian Federal Provincial Conference in July 1965. The federal government had decided to refer to the Supreme Court the question of title to sea-bed resources on the Pacific Coast, but the premiers of British Columbia and of Quebec "led a furious attack on the federal government, claiming that the matter was one for political negotiations and not for judicial settlement." The premier of Quebec declared that he would not respect a supreme court decision, or allow exploration in the Gulf of St. Lawrence on the strength of a federal permit (*The Guardian,* London, July 24, 1965).

open the door for "any European country" willing to join implies, according to Mr. Nederhorst, full acceptance of "existing economic institutions and political principles"; and it was not unnatural in the discussions on the Fouchet plan for the French to insist there, too, on unanimity for new admissions. As under the Rome Treaty the Commission has a prominent voice in this matter, there is much to be learned from the remarkable change of mind from its memorandum of February 1959, which urged "very great flexibility" so as to allow "association" according to the needs and wishes of any likely candidate, to its recent hardened position against anything short of full membership.

On a minor scale the contrast stands out clearly even within the existing communities. The ECSC and Euratom are straight functional bodies and can get on with their allotted task without offending the position of other countries, while remaining open to link up with them. The scope of EEC is by comparison diffuse and subject to a continuous temptation to self-inflation (which the "Europeans" deem a virtue), with a bureaucratic tendency because it is diffuse and an expansionist tendency because it is bureaucratic. The more fields of activity it actively enters, e.g., agriculture, the more acquisitive it tends to become;[16] and in the degree to which it is rounded out it also hardens into a segregated entity. (One might have predicted this even without the repulsion of the Seven into the EFTA grouping, and without the later rupture of negotiations with Great Britain.) The point is that for service units like the ECSC and Euratom, as for all the specialized agencies of the U.N. and any future functional bodies, wider association means

[16] "The General, despite his dislike of integration, has done much to reinforce the Commission's powers, by pressing for a common agricultural policy which it alone can administer." On its part, using the argument that it would be undemocratic to handle the large agricultural funds without democratic control, the Commission has put forward a scheme "which would transfer much of the Council's powers to the Parliament, and, even more, to the Commission." *The Economist,* London, May 8, 1965, p. 638.

more points of co-operative contact; for a self-inflating organization like the EEC, more fields of control must mean internationally more points of competitive contact.

Federation was an advance on empire as a way of joining under a common government a group of separate territorial units. But federation is not only inadequate but irrelevant when the general task is not to consolidate but to loosen the hold of the territorially sovereign conception of political relations and find a way to world peace through the revolutionary pressures of the time. Even earlier neither the British Empire nor Latin America, with their many social and historical affinities, had turned to the federal idea for political comfort.[17] It has not served any of the post-war problems and situations. It has not proved acceptable to neighboring groups in East Africa or the Middle East or the Caribbean in spite of pressing common needs and paucity of resources; alone the Nigerian federation survives, not too easily, in the wake of a unitary administration. It has not suggested itself as a remedy for healing the split between parts that had been formerly united. Some years ago Mr. Nehru and the Pakistani president agreed that their countries had many practical interests which could with advantage be managed in common, and now the leaders of the two parts of

---

[17] In reviewing *The Failure of Union: Central America, 1824-1960* by Thomas L. Karnes (Chapel Hill, 1961), Miguel Wionczek suggested that "the failure to unify Central America over more than a century was mainly due to a wrong approach of making political federation the exclusive goal. But once the political status quo had been accepted . . . very considerable progress was registered in a relatively short period of time in the field of economic cooperation"; and "many other possibilities of cooperation are discovered gradually and in spite of continuous political division and sporadic frictions. . . ." (*Journal of Common Market Studies,* December 1965, p. 193.) In Europe, "it is characteristic of Nordic cooperative endeavors that they avoid all political abstractions and all speculations regarding final goals. Rather they aim at the solving of concrete, practical problems, advancing step by step and accepting gladly every conquest, no matter how small" (*Danish Foreign Office Periodical,* March 2, 1956), not only in economic but also in cultural and welfare matters.

Ireland are working to end an old enmity by doing just that. But would either case have had a better prospect if one of the parties were to have said, "We must federate first"? Quite a number of practical activities are carried out in common by or for the British Commonwealth, but would any mere hint that they needed a political underpinning not cause at once a flight from this functional association?

When it comes to the new scientific inventions and discoveries —aviation, communications, atomic energy, space exploration— their own technicalities defy any arrangement below the global scale. So much so that, e.g., in broadcasting, states have to respect the mutual interest even where there is no formal agreement. Flying may still claim for a while sovereign rights in the air above a state's territory; but with satellites and space travel we have in truth reached the "no man's land of sovereignty." Nor is there any workable dividing line between military and non-military usage of space; no means of self-protection is left, only all-round protection through some common authority. The program for space exploration adopted by the General Assembly in 1962 was only a first step toward taking it out of politics; and the same intent clearly informed the Antarctica Treaty signed by twelve countries, including Soviet Russia, in 1959, which suspended all territorial claims and disputes for a period of thirty years and instead provided for scientific co-operation and also for mutual inspection to prevent any military activities. These are, if one may be allowed the expression, not federalizing but functionalizing actions; they could never lead to federation between the parties, but the Antarctica Treaty—considered as a type—which now amounts to a temporary neutralization under a joint agreement, could well lead to permanent neutralization under a joint international authority.

Before concluding, there are two points that need to be mentioned, as they recur in almost every critical account of the functional approach. One is the central difficult question of co-ordination. To a degree, insofar as it is raised as an abstract assumption, it expresses the difficulty which our political thinking finds in conceiving of authority, as part of the tradition of sovereignty, without a territory; even the Roman pontiff had to be allowed the Vatican territory as a base for sovereign status, though it is less than a speck on the pontiff's vast expanse of influence and authority throughout the world. But the criticism also has a core of evident truth in the fear that a variety of autonomous organs might work at cross-purposes with each other. It is a real problem, but is it not better to wait till the need arises and experience shows what the need is? To prescribe for the sake of traditional neatness something more definite than the guidance and supervision of, e.g., the Economic and Social Council, would be to distort the whole conception from the start. To try to fit the functional bodies into a common mold would take away some of their special merits in working efficiency and flexibility of membership; while to impose upon them a co-ordinating authority, with anything like controlling status, would be to move again toward that accumulation of power at the center which is in question here. We would be drifting back onto the political track and so miss the way to possible universality.

The second point is one of doubt, not infrequently heard: "Where will the political will for such functional union come from?" It seems a curious question. If there should be no will for working together on such lines, limited to evident self-interest, can one assume that there might be a better will for wider unlimited political integration? The question is not so much a criticism of the functional idea as a great doubt whether peaceful international co-operation is possible at all. It is perhaps an open question whether in 1945 we had been too hopeful or too form-bound in our approach. In the view of Senator J. W. Fulbright, the U.N. has in a manner broken down because it was based on the assumption of a unity of outlook among the Great Powers; now we have to turn to a functional approach to build up an international community, to tackle concrete problems instead of spectacular attempts at world constitution-making. The same question, whether they were too hopeful or too form-tied, applies to the "Europeans" who gathered at The Hague in 1948. Many of them now feel the need for "a more cautious conception of integration," to quote Professor von Geusau again; "if Europe is to pursue its fundamental goal, functional integration appears to be the only practical method of cooperation." And the fundamental goal here means not local peace and strength, but world peace and well-being. As to this ultimate goal, in the concluding volume of the series of inquiries initiated by the Carnegie Endowment for International Peace, *The Nations and the United Nations,* Professor Robert MacIver himself concluded that the U.N.'s main service to the cause of peace may lie not in its political activities, but in the development of the common or cooperative interests of the peoples in areas which lie outside, or on the margin of, the usual play of power politics.

INDEX

216

216 INDEX

Economic parliaments, failure, 125-126, 206fn

Equality: evolution within states, 104-105; internationally, 105ff; real vs. formal, 120, 144

Equality of states, 105ff, 144; legal equality, 105; political equality, 106; social equality, 117; through common services, 66ff, 80-81; of representation, 119

Equity tribunals, 35

European Coal and Steel Community (ECSC): equality of members, 111; functional parliament in, 110, 125; and social equality, 115; as supra-national agency, 116, 207

European Union: European Economic Community (Common Market), 174-213; anti-USSR, anti-U.S., 181, 184; Briand scheme, 188; civilization, open, 185; Communists excluded, 197-198; coincides with decline of Europe's power, 182; contrast with *Federalist*, 174-175; vagueness of political idea, 176-179, 191-192; economic fallacy, 183; federal fallacy, 187ff; functional way, 213; Parliament, 195; political approach, 177-178; union narrowing, 179-180; regional approach, 180ff

Federal Commerce Commission (U.S.), 74

Federalism (federation): as alternative to League of Nations, 36-38; closed and exclusive, 208-209; constitutions conservative and legalistic, 153-154; rigid, obstacle to social change, 32-33, 52, 154-156, 157-159, 172-173, 189, 203; TVA, 171; dialectical confusion,

169; difficulties, 27, 82, 208fn; helped by international commitments, 189; difficulties of international federations, 151-157; distinction from functional (Lange), 170; failure of schemes for, 16, 17, 20, 90, 210, 210fn; after World War, 36-37; as index of power, 159; international, 152-153; mutually exclusive, 162; and planning, 52, 156; problems of, 43-54; purpose of, 152, 156; secession, threats of, 189

Federalism, "functional," 167ff

"Federalizing" process (Prof. Carl Friedrich), 190-192; peculiar *Way of Federalism* (Denis de Rougemont), 169

Fichte, *Der Geschlossene Handelstaat,* 200

"Foreign Aid." *See* Technical Assistance.

Functionalism: acceptance by new states, 18, 165; advantages, social and economic, 160; and church unity, 161; over political forms (Burke), 150, 163; only reply to nationalism, 10-11; and future of world, 11; in administrative law and practice, 19, 137; co-ordination, 73ff, 137-138, 140, 211-212; definition, 161; original formulation, 20; philosophy of, 204; new outlook, not device, 18-19, 164; democratic participation, 49-50, 64-66, 77ff, 83-84, 205, 207; equality of states, 63, 68; and federation (Lange), 170; in federations, 57-58, 82-83, 157-158; between federations, 158-159, 168; cp. with federalism, 54ff; Fulbright, Senator J. W., on need of functional action, 212; functional

International Federation of Trade
Unions, 90
International labor relations, through
functionalism, 90
International law: functional development, 201; limitations of judiciary, 146; role in nineteenth
century, 40, 113
International organization: desire
for, 150; difficulty of changing
constitution, 32; based on functionalism, 163; three types, 27,
151
International police force, anachronism, 61
International relations: democratic
test, 49-50; diplomatic evolution
(technical decentralization), 63,
131, 133-137, 207
International society: achievement
of, through functional action, 81-
99; through everyday co-operation, 146; development in nineteenth century, 108, 111; contrast
with twentieth century, 155; ends
of, 35, 55; growth of idea of, 31;
League of Nations reconstruction
loans still nationalistic, 131; need
for fresh methods to achieve, 38-
39; purpose of any new system,
48; U.N. and progress toward,
115, 134-135
Ireland, steps to end old enmity in,
16

Japan: and "continental" unions,
44; "co-prosperity sphere," 29;
and League of Nations and ILO,
49, 83
John XXIII, Pope, *Pacem in Terris*
encyclical and "peaceful coexistence," 14-15

Kellogg Pact, 42
Khrushchev, Nikita, definition of
"coexistence," 14

Labor relations, international,
through functionalism, 90
Lange, M. H. M., and European
union, 170
Latin America: political ambitions
and divisions, 16; federal failure
and functional success, 210fn; and
League of Nations, 53; and Pan-
Americanism, 53
Layton, Lord, on British opinion on
European union, 171
League of Nations, 28; amendments
to constitution, 33; Bruce Report
(1939), 115fn; Covenant in nineteenth century tradition, 40, 55,
60; economic co-operation, 136;
failures and frustrations of, 34,
36-37, 40, 41, 42, 55, 60; Japan
and, 49, 83; minorities and mandates systems, 113-114; nationalist outlook of, 131; and national
separateness, 151; and regional
unions, 188; service unions, 115;
and social and economic services,
114; USSR and, 49
League of Nations Covenant: and
equality of states, 103; House-
Wilson draft, 109; Hurst-Miller
draft, 109; territorial revision, 107
League of "peoples," 33-34, 43-44
Locarno Pact, 42

Mandates system, 113-114
Marshall Plan, 160
Menzies, R., on British Common-
wealth, 171
Middle East: schemes for federa-
tion, 16; and self-government,

A NOTE ON THE AUTHOR

David Mitrany was born in Bucharest, studied for short
periods in Paris and Hamburg, and received his degrees
from the University of London (School of Economics).
He was professor in the School of Economics and Politics at the Institute for Advanced Study, Princeton, from
its beginning in 1933, and the first Permanent Member
of the Institute. He has also taught in the United States
at Harvard, Yale, and Smith, and has served in England
on the editorial staff of the *Manchester Guardian*. Of his
several books, the best known is *Marx Against the
Peasant*. Professor Mitrany now lives in Oxford,
England.